Blo

BLOODY LUCKY

Writing on Cricket

EDITED BY

TOM GRAVENEY AND MIKE SEABROOK

ILLUSTRATED BY

BILL TIDY

P O C K E T B O O K S

LONDON·SYDNEY·NEW YORK·TOKYO·SINGAPORE·TORONTO

First published in Great Britain by
Simon & Schuster Ltd, 1990
First published in Great Britain by Pocket Books, 1994
An imprint of Simon & Schuster Ltd
A Paramount Communications Company

Simon & Schuster Ltd
West Garden Place
Kendal Street
London W2 2AQ

Simon & Schuster of Australia Pty Ltd
Sydney

A CIP catalogue record for this book is
available from the British Library

ISBN 0-671-85311-2

Typeset in Sabon 10.5/12.5pt by
Hewer Text Composition Services, Edinburgh
Printed and bound in Great Britain by
Harper*Collins* Manufacturing, Glasgow

Contents

ABOUT THE CONTRIBUTORS vii

INTRODUCTION 1

BLOODY LUCKY *Stephen Fry* 9

THE FIRST SATURDAY IN MAY *J. L. Carr* 32

ROUNDHEAD CRICKET *Edward Pearce* 40

CRICKET, LOVELY CRICKET *Frederic Raphael* 50

IT'S MANNERS THAT HAVE CHANGED
C. H. Rolph 67

LES TAYLOR *Martin Johnson* 77

CONFESSIONS OF A CRICKETER *Mike Brearley* 83

TOOTHLE *Bill Tidy* 114

KNOWN FOR THE BEST *John Arlott* 125

THE CASE OF THE DISAPPEARING AUDIENCE
Miles Kington 139

CONTENTS

PRIME MINISTER RESHUFFLES
The Hon. Michael Manley 149

LORD'S *Tom Gravney* 156

YOU CAN TAKE GLORY WITH YOU
Michael Jayston 160

MR AND MRS FRY *Richard Gordon* 177

STYLE *Alan Ross* 186

CRICKET ON ELYSIAN FIELDS
John Holmstrom 191

A LATE INNINGS *Ian Wallace* 202

THE USE OF MEMORY *Trevor McDonald* 213

BOB CAUGHT CAROL BOWLED ALICE
Mark Lawson 221

RETIRED HURT *Donald Trelford* 246

LET THEM EAT CAKE *Edwing Brock* 255

THE SOUTHERN DRIFTERS *David English* 260

DID GEORGE ORWELL GET IT RIGHT?
John Timpson 266

BOWLED OVER *Brian Walden* 273

UNMIXED BLESSINGS *Mike Seabrook* 285

About the Contributors

John Arlott was for many years the voice of cricket, his broadcasting style as unique as his voice. In addition to commentating, he has written many books on the game. He also broadcast regularly (*Any Questions?* etc.), served as a police officer, stood as a Liberal parliamentary candidate and for many years wrote for the *Guardian* on wine. He spent his last years in Alderney, where he died at the age of 77 in 1991. His contribution to this book was, we believe, the last essay he wrote on the game that had been the great love of his life, and to which he had contributed so much.

Mike Brearley played for Middlesex from 1962 to 1982, and for England from 1976 to 1981, including two spells as captain, in which role he was by common consent the most intelligent and inspirational figure for decades. During that period he also spent four years as a lecturer in philosophy at Newcastle-upon-Tyne. He has written extensively about cricket.

EDWIN BROCK has been a sailor, a London policeman and an award-winning advertising copywriter. He made the headlines when he published the first of ten collections of poetry while still serving in the police. His latest collection of new and selected poems, *Five Ways To Kill A Man*, appeared in 1990.

JAMES CARR of Kettering is a publisher, famous for his series of pocket-sized introductions to poetry, historical figures and miscellaneous matters. He is also the author of several idiosyncratic novels, among the best-known being *The Battle of Pollock's Crossing* and *A Month in the Country*, which won the *Guardian* Fiction Prize and was nominated for the Booker Prize.

DAVID ENGLISH managed Eric Clapton and the Bee Gees, and is now an actor. He is also a well-known humorist, stalwart of Finchley CC and author of the *Bunbury Tails*, his series of adventures of the famous cricketing rabbits.

STEPHEN FRY is an actor, mostly in comic roles (*This is David Lander*, *Blackadder*, *Jeeves and Wooster* etc.), a comedian (*A Bit of Fry and Laurie*, etc.) and writer. His column for *The Listener* was highly praised. His first novel, *The Liar*, was published in 1991, and included a modified version of the hilarious cricket story that he contributed to this book.

RICHARD GORDON is the pseudonym of Dr Gordon Ostlere. He has been at various times anaesthetist at St Bartholomew's Hospital, assistant editor of the British Medical Journal, a ship's surgeon, and the author of the famous 'Doctor in the House' series of books, many of which have been made into comedy films. His most recent book is a scholarly, acerbic and very funny history of medical practice in its murkier and less heroic aspects.

TOM GRAVENEY is one of England's finest post-war cricketers. He played for Gloucestershire, then Worcestershire, from 1949 to 1970, and for England in 79 Tests, in which he scored nearly 5,000 runs, with a highest score of 258 against the West Indies. He became a by-word for grace and elegance of strokeplay. He is now a television cricket commentator with a nice line in dry wit.

JOHN HOLMSTROM was for many years what Americans would call the 'anchorman' of BBC Radio 3, where his mellifluous voice, quick wit and genial imperturbability won him a large personal following. He once announced that the news was cancelled for the day 'because I've lost it'. He was born in Yorkshire, and now lives in retirement in North London, where he and a circle of friends have formed a complicated computer cricket league.

MICHAEL JAYSTON is one of Britain's best-known actors. He has been a member of the Royal Shakespeare Company, and played many roles on television from the upwardly mobile young executive in *The Power Game* to Alec Guinness's trusted assistant spycatcher in *Tinker, Tailor, Soldier, Spy*.

MARTIN JOHNSON was for many years cricket and rugby correspondent for the *Leicester Mercury*, before taking up the cricket post on the *Independent* on the paper's launch. Since then he has won great acclaim for his trenchant and often hilarious style – he is even read widely by those who are otherwise uninterested in the game. He contributed a particularly witty essay to Mike Seabrook's authology of golf writing, *One Over Par* (1993).

MILES KINGTON is a former editor of *Punch*, inventor of the famous *Let's speak Franglais* column and television wit. In recent years he has written a daily column for the *Independent*, where he has established himself as contemporary journalism's only serious challenger for the mantle of the late and still-lamented Beachcomber. He was a contributor to *One Over Par*.

MARK LAWSON is yet another of the generation of

sharp wits and lively prose stylists who blossomed with the arrival of the *Independent*, first as television correspondent, then doubling, for all too short a period, as parliamentary sketch writer; he now writes for the weekend magazine.

MICHAEL MANLEY was Prime Minister of Jamaica from 1972 to 1980 and again from 1989 until his retirement in 1992. He had been MP for Central Kingston since 1967 and President of the People's National Party since 1969. While leading the opposition he found time to write a monumental history of West Indian cricket; he has also written widely on Caribbean politics, and received numerous political honours worldwide.

TREVOR MCDONALD is a senior newscaster and journalist with Independent Television News, and one of the most familiar faces on ITV and Channel Four. Among his writings is a biography of Vivian Richards. His autobiography was published in 1993.

EDWARD PEARCE has been parliamentary sketch writer for the *Daily Telegraph*, a columnist on the *Sunday Times*, and 'Cross-Bencher' for the *Sunday Express*. He writes opera and theatre criticism, has a regular column in the *Guardian*, and has written four mordant and very funny books of contemporary political analysis, a biography of John Major and an on-the-stump diary of the electioneering campaign of 1992. His most recent book, *Machiavelli's Children*, presents the political philosopher's ideas, updated for modern readers. He is working on a novel.

FREDERIC RAPHAEL is one of the leading writers of his generation, with many novels, collections of short stories, biographies, screenplays and translations from Latin and Greek literature to his credit. His series of TV plays adapted from his own novel *The Glittering Prizes* won him the award as Writer of the Year from the Royal Television Society in 1976.

C.H. ROLPH has been writing, mainly about the law, for well over 50 years. He has been a director of the *New Statesman*, worked for the Society of Authors and the Howard League for Penal Reform, and written some thirty books of legal analysis, biography and autobiography. His column in the weekly magazine *Police Review* has been running continually for 60 years, which is the world record.

ALAN ROSS is an author, poet, journalist and publisher, with over thirty books of all kinds to his name, including many collections of poems. He has for many years edited the *London Magazine*, was a columnist on *The Observer* for over 20 years, and has produced numerous books on cricket, which he played for Oxford University and the Royal Navy.

MIKE SEABROOK writes novels and non-fiction. His books include *Coppers*, a study of the police, in which he served for a time, three highly controversial novels, and various others, including two on cricket. His biography of the composer Sir Peter Maxwell Davies will appear in 1994, together with another novel and a collection of essays on horse racing. He writes for various periodicals, on the law, cricket and music.

BILL TIDY is one of Britain's best-known cartoonists, who has worked in virtually every prominent publication in the country. He appears frequently on television, where he exercises his fondness for games programmes – the whimsical sense of humour that informs his cartoons regularly enlivens Channel Four's popular *Countdown* series.

JOHN TIMPSON has spent a lifetime in local and national journalism, radio and television. He is probably best known from his marathon spell as one of the co-presenters of Radio 4's breakfast programme *Today*.

DONALD TRELFORD was editor of the *Observer* for many years, and a journalist all his working life, much of it in Africa. He played rugby and cricket for Cambridge, plays golf and snooker, and has written a highly amusing book, *Snookered*, about the latter. He is a member of the Committee of MCC.

Brian Walden was Labour MP for the All Saints and Ladywood constituencies in Birmingham from 1964 to 1977, when he resigned to take over *Weekend World*, ITV's flagship current affairs programme. He still interviews the wielders of power on TV, and writes an outspoken column in the *Sunday Times*.

Ian Wallace sang many comic baritone roles in a long operatic career, especially as a stalwart of Glyndebourne. At the same time he broadcast regularly, as singer, actor, compère and wit, in particular on the long-running radio and TV panel game *My Music*. Though from a non-cricketing background, he fell in love with the game as a boy at Charterhouse.

Introduction

IF A RANDOM sample of Americans-in-the street were asked to suggest a handful of images that epitomised England, we could safely expect them to include, along with royalty, the Tower of London and Big Ben, a number of familiar rural scenes. There would be a hunt meeting on a crisp, frosty morning on some archetypal village green, complete with Queen Anne houses, immemorial elms and vaguely eighteenth-century figures in hunting pink, taking the stirrup cup outside an oakery-beamery country inn; for the aurally suggestible there might be the sound of churchbells floating across the same village green, summoning the local rustics to prayer in the picture-postcard mediaeval church; and, in all probability, they would suggest also a vision of white-clad figures flitting hither and thither across the same green, taking part in the mystique-shrouded, but powerfully evocative ritual of cricket.

These images have become a sort of code, or shorthand

– what a contemporary ad exec might describe as part of the sales package – for England as she is to be marketed to tourists.

The thing to be remembered, of course, is that this England does not exist, and, to be honest, probably never did. The tourist adventurous enough to go in search of that wonderful rustic pub with its ancient oaken beams and the row of yokels, becorduroyed and pipesmoking as they quaff their foaming tankards of ale, will find . . . well, we know what he'll find. Across the green, the church is most likely falling down, boarded up or both. The hunt may be picturesque enough, but it is equally likely to turn into a kind of Battle of the Somme in miniature, with more hunt saboteurs chasing huntsmen than hounds chasing foxes.

It's rather hard luck on our American that amid all this prevailing disillusion the one archetype – 'stereotype' is perhaps too negative a word – which still manages to retain some of its truth is the one he is least likely to find easily assimilable. None the less, cricket is the one among these metaphors for Old England which can legitimately claim not only to have once possessed some of the virtues its lovers ascribe to it, but also to possess the same virtues in good measure to this day. Many whom the game has failed to touch get quite angry about what they regard as the extravagant claims made for it by its devotees; but the devotee can claim, with a good deal of evidence to justify it, that the game does remain generally good-natured, generous and kind-hearted.

The opposition can, of course, point to examples where it has gone sour, where the nastier manifestations of money-grubbing have seeped in from other professional sport; they can point to public exhibitions of drunkenness and cretinous chanting, and so on. But there is little of this, and at the points at which most cricket-lovers make their personal contact with the game – at village, club and minor counties levels – there is none of it at all.

That said, a case can be made – is made, often, by the game's detractors – that in the literature of the game (it remains virtually alone among sports in supporting a profuse and genuine literature) the tendency towards wishful thinking, towards a rosy-tinted nostalgia that is essentially bogus, is altogether too prevalent. This book is the refutation of that charge.

Within the twenty-odd pieces in this collection, the true cricket-lover will find every facet of the game represented. The result is that the game appears whole, and therefore unfaked by the distorting-glass of nostalgia or self-delusion. And since when the reader has digested all the contributions he will, we feel confident, come away with a favourable, friendly impression of the game, that is the evidence we offer that the game itself remains healthy, sane and uplifting. It does, actually, deliver the joy, the friendship and the fun it promises, rather than promising only to deceive and disappoint.

None of this is to say that there is no truth in the

nostalgic recollection of golden days in the sun. James Carr writes tenderly of an age that has vanished, with steam trains, and enough of a rail network for them to run on to make it imaginable that a cricket team might travel to an away match by rail. His picture of the West Midlands is as evocative as Housman, and in some ways more authentic because more human.

Michael Jayston also looks back at the traditions of the game, and finds that standards of conduct and manners have deteriorated; but the relish with which he enlivens his reflections with some salty anecdotes demonstrates convincingly that his affection for the game is undiminished. John Arlott, who is, well within his own lifetime, a tradition of the game himself, reviews some of the very best of the vast array of great players he has seen in a long lifetime of cricket, and he does so, typically, with enormous warmth but without sentimentality. C.H. Rolph, too, compares contemporary manners with those of an earlier era, spicing his writing, as he has spiced his observations on the police and the law these sixty years past, with wit and erudition; and once again, the fact that he still wishes to write with grace and style about the game betrays the continuing fondness he harbours for it.

So, yes, of course there is some truth to be found in looking backwards. It's just that nostalgia doesn't offer the *only* truth about the game. If ever a cricketer's captaincy could properly be described as inspired, Mike Brearley's could. Here he writes with the same penetrating intelligence that informed his cricket about the psychology of the game, the difficulties of captaincy and the relationships that this most complex and fascinating of games breeds. Nothing could be more up-to-date, less backward-looking, than this.

As none knows better than Mike Brearley, if cricket is generally benign and good-humoured, it can sometimes be the opposite: a cruel excoriation of the soul, a dissection of a man's character made so much the more pitiless for being conducted in full public glare. Brian Walden turns a customarily baleful gaze and uncompromising prose style on the cruel face of modern international cricket here. Mark Lawson also writes of cricket as a microcosm of life in its less merciful aspects, in a very different setting, on a Devon beach. For startingly vivid contrast, try Frederic Raphael's almost cinematic treatment of love and cricket entwined on other beaches.

Mark Lawson's contribution represents one of the departures we are most proud of in this collection: the revival of the short story on a cricketing theme. There are two others here: we present what we believe is a world first – a cricketing murder mystery, from Miles Kington, the latter-day Beachcomber; and Stephen Fry offers what is perhaps the funniest cricketing tale since the legendary village match in A.G. Macdonnell's *England, Their England.*

If cricket is of all games the one with the greatest humanity, it is humour, of course, that makes it so. Edwin Brock gently satirises the cake-eating heroes of BBC radio's Test Match Special; John Holmstrom, whose much-loved voice ushered those immortals into our living rooms for so many years, writes entertainingly about the delights of computerised cricket; Bill Tidy, whose illustrations enliven the whole collection, also contributes a typical piece of whimsy, like one of his own cartoons translated into words; David English looks back happily on deplorable goings-on on tour in the Caribbean; and Martin Johnson, the funniest of all newspaper cricket correspondents, laughs with reverence and affection at a Leicestershire hero.

Heroes are another commodity that the game abounds in, and there are plenty here. John Arlott's selection has been mentioned. Michael Manley of Jamaica (who must be the only Prime Minister with a monumental book of cricket history to his credit) indulges in that most pleasurable pastime for the true cricket lunatic in the cold exile of winter, picking the greatest-of-all-time team – in his case, needless to say, the champion of champions West Indian side, and Trevor McDonald recalls two of the greatest Caribbean cricketers of all. Alan Ross, too, devotes his essay to a discussion of what constitutes 'style', that quality in a cricketer that sets him apart from all others of equal or even superior talent, so difficult to define yet so unmistakably recognisable when it is seen. Finally, for piquancy, Richard Gordon presents an iconoclastic portrait of one of England cricket's all-time heroes, shown here as you've *never* seen him before.

The list is rounded off as we began, with reminiscence – and this is something that all cricket-lovers, everywhere, indulge in. You can do it alone or in company. You can do it in bed or by the fire, or you can slip into a reverie for a while when the office or the factory, the House of Lords or Commons, the policeman's beat or the building site becomes too awful to tolerate. Ian Wallace looks back to a memorable game against a team of blind cricketers – surely the greatest tribute to the game, as well as to the unimaginable courage and dedication of the people involved. John Timpson casts a wry glance back to his schooldays, the source of fond memories for Donald Trelford too, in the course of a happy cricketing life. Edward Pearce draws on a variety of sources for his prescription for the game of the future: a classic cricket story of the golden age, one of the greatest, perhaps *the* greatest English hero of them all, and his own boyhood in the tough industrial north, and then brings us right up to date.

Finally, we, the editors, were unable to resist the temptation to add our own offerings. Tom Graveney writes about Lord's – the innermost sanctum of the game, the shrine to which every cricketer in the world must journey once, the place where the Laws are made, or, simply, 'headquarters'. Mike Seabrook also speaks with reverence of the holy place, in the course of a pleasurable ramble which finds room for Ian Botham and North Mymms, Sir Isaac Newton and Sir Alastair Burnet.

Emotion and reflection, nostalgia and pugnacity, competitiveness and friendship, heroes and the occasional villain, and above all humour, fun and kindness, leavened by occasional life-reflecting cruelty – such is cricket. It remains of all games the one that can inspire the profoundest and most tenacious devotion, simply because of all games it is the closest in its patterns to life itself, embodies the broadest range of humanity and humanity's emotions. Of all games it comes by far the closest to an art form – both in this reflection of humanity and life, and in its beautiful patterns of white on green, its harmonies and dissonances.

Writing, too, of course, is art, of the highest. Some people fall, headlong and forever, under cricket's spell; some remain forever immune to its charms. Some people can write; most people can't. This collection of essays shows the fusion of the two arts at its happiest and best.

Bloody Lucky

STEPHEN FRY

THREE OF US, at school, Richard Waters, Tom Downey and myself. We're far away in the days before girls had been invented, the days before schools were encouraged to train the young for examinations, industry and responsibility, the days before global warming caused that distasteful phenomenon of precipitated water droplets that we now know as rain. We are, in fact, deep in the heart of 1971. I am thirteen and the world is a compound of pure sunshine, Led Zeppelin, Monty Python and Alan Knott.

Richard Waters was the most talented schoolboy batsman in England, the Peter May *de nos jours*. Tom Downey bowled the competent high looping leg-breaks that only schoolboys can bowl and was a natural musician of great flair and panache. I lumbered and loomed around the cricket field for the Third Eleven Colts like an injured ostrich, here dropping a catch, there bowling slow full-tosses and delicious half-volleys that made

Bradmen of the naffest tail-enders. I wrote comedy sketches though, acted in plays and did a marvellous imitation of Oliver Postgate, the narrator of *Noggin the Nog* and *The Clangers*, so life was not all misery.

Whenever the school First Eleven played a match and the Colts had no fixture, I was asked to be the scorer. I would perch on a table at the front of the pavilion, next to whichever wheezy and pustular freak the visiting school had supplied to score for them, and watch my two best friends out in the middle. My bowels would churn and boil with despairing envy as Richard Waters sent his liquid left-handed drives to the boundary. Waves of frantic jealousy would cause the sweat to break out on my forehead when he hitched up his flannels at the knees before bending brightly in the slips. The sight of Tom licking the ring finger of his right hand as he prepared to wheel in his flippers and bouncing leg-breaks made me choke with anger and greed. They're just so lucky. So bloody lucky. Lucky, lucky, lucky.

They both had the one thing in the world I most wanted: skill at cricket. I couldn't bear it. I was like a beached puffin gazing up at the gulls. Each night I would lie awake playing a film over and over to myself, a film which starred me as First Eleven Opening Bat, Worcestershire Opening Bat and finally, triumphantly, England Opening Bat. If I wished hard enough, if my prayers battered at the gates of heaven loudly enough, they would be answered. Just enough talent to make me a player, that's all I required. I would give up all the rest of my life just to have the chance to spend twenty years as a professional cricketer. The rest: academic ability, a mimetic voice, the talent to write plausible essays, they could all take a flying shag as far as I was concerned. Cricket: that was all that mattered and all that ever could. I was so unlucky, so bloody unlucky. It wasn't fair. It just wasn't. God, I was unlucky.

We were sixteen when Tom announced one afternoon in the Lower Buttery that he was giving up cricket to concentrate on the band that he and a couple of weird friends from another House were forming.

'What! Are you out of your frigging mind?' I screamed.

'That's odd, I was just about to award you your colours,' said Richard.

'The thing of it is,' said Tom, 'Grey told me that next time I played I would have to cut my hair.'

'And that's the reason, is it?' I cried, revolted. 'You could be a county player one day, you know that?'

'The band's the thing.'

Richard and I talked about it in our study that night.

'He's mad,' I said. 'He's off his sodding head.'

'He's our only leg-spinner, more's the point,' said Richard. 'Anyway, this bloody essay, what does it mean, "Macbeth: the microcosm and the macrocosm. Discuss." *Discuss*? Discuss what?'

By the end of that term my housemaster had had enough of me. 'We don't want you back, boy. No, we don't. You're either going to become a criminal mastermind or Prime Minister of this country. I hope to God for all our sakes that it's the former.'

'Well, sir,' I said, 'if I do become Prime Minister I promise I'll forgive you and the school everything.'

'Oh go away, just go away. Come back and see me when you've got a soul.'

After a series of adventures, of which the details have no place in a cricketing memoir, I was awarded a scholarship to St Matthew's College, Cambridge to read English.

I decided to fill my gap, that period between acceptance by a university and actually going up, by teaching at a prep school in the approved Paul Pennyfeather and W.H. Auden fashion. Chartham Park in Norfolk called me and I answered the call gladly.

'We particularly need someone to look after the cricket, which will be in disarray,' the headmaster had told me. 'Our cricket man, the man you're replacing, had to . . . erm . . . he had to leave.'

'Oh,' I asked innocently, 'why?'

'Illness,' said the headmaster firmly.

'Really?' I said. 'How shocking. I hope you managed to hush it up.'

The atmosphere in the minibus was tense. I sat with the boys and tried to look sunny and confident. But it was no good my telling them it was only a game when I was so nervous myself.

'We'll take a look at the pitch,' I told Hooper, the Captain, 'and we'll decide then. But unless it's decidedly moist, put them in the field if you win the

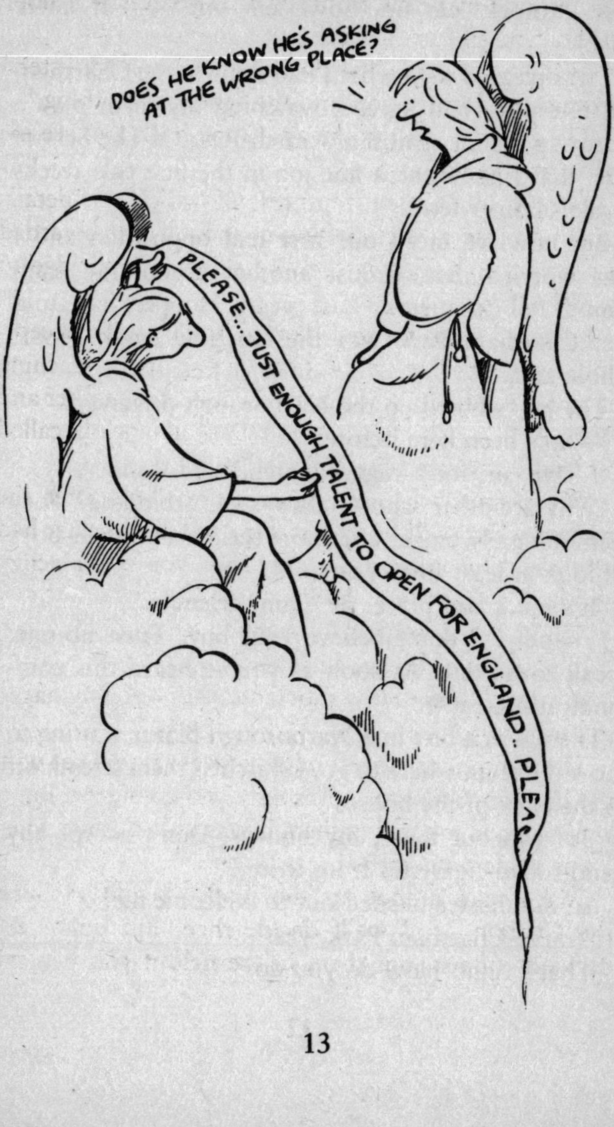
DOES HE KNOW HE'S ASKING AT THE WRONG PLACE?
PLEASE... JUST ENOUGH TALENT TO OPEN FOR ENGLAND.. PLEAS

toss. "Knock 'em up, bowl 'em out" . . . it never fails.'

I was pleased with what I had done to the Chartham XI. Everyone had agreed, watching my team play a warm-up match against a scratch Rest Of The School side, that I had done a fine job in the first two weeks of the summer term.

But now we faced our first real opposition and I was worried that against another school my team would fall to pieces. Last year, Hooper had told me, Chartham Park was the laughing stock of the whole area.

The bus whined up the Narborough driveway.

'Who's been here before?'

'I have, sir, for a rugger match,' said Rudder.

'Why are other schools always so forbidding? They seem infinitely bigger and more serious and their boys all look at least forty years old.'

'It's not a bad place, sir. Quite friendly.'

'Friendly? I don't believe you, boy. Trust no-one, speak to no-one. As soon as you've heard this communication, eat it.'

There was a boy in a Narborough blazer waiting to show the team where to go. I watched them stream off to the back of the house.

'See you out there, my honeys. Don't accept any hand-rolled cigarettes from them.'

An old master bustled out to welcome me.

'You're Chartham Park, yes?'

'That's right. How do you do?'

'Staveley. I'm not cricket. Our cricket man's giving the team a pep talk. It's morning break at the moment. Come through to the staff room and savage a chelsea bun with us.'

The staff room was baronial and crowded with what seemed to me like a greater number of masters than Chartham had boys.

'Ah, Chartham's new blood!' boomed the headmaster. 'Come to give us a spanking, have you?'

'Oh, well, I don't know about that, sir.' I shook his hand. 'They tell me that you're hot stuff. Double figures would satisfy us.'

'That false modesty doesn't do, you know. I can smell your confidence. You're St Matthew's bound, I understand?'

'That's right, sir.'

'Well, then, you'll be pleased to meet my uncle Donald who's staying here until Cambridge term begins. He'll be your Senior Tutor of course. Where is he? Uncle Donald, meet Chartham Park's new secret weapon, he's joining you at Michaelmas.'

A short man with grey hair and a startled expression turned and surveyed me. This was the famous Donald Trefusis.

'Ah, yes, yes indeed. How do you do?'

'How do you do, Professor?'

'Yes, that's right. Quite right. Your entrance paper was very encouraging. I remember it well. Pregnant with promise, gravid with wit.'

'Thank you.'

'And you're a cricketer?'

'Well, not really. I've been trying to coach a bit, though.'

'Well, best of luck, my dear. My nephew Philip has a youth like yourself on the staff – he'll be going to Trinity – who is said to have done much with the Narborough side. Quite the young thaumaturge, they tell me. Here he comes now, you'll be umpiring together. Let me introduce you.'

I turned to see a young man in a cricket sweater making his way towards us.

Well, well, well. Well, well, *well*, well, well.

'I already know Richard Waters,' I said. 'We were at school together.'

'Hello,' said Richard.'Ready to be pounded into the dust?'

We put on our white coats and walked down to the ground.'What sort of a wicket have you got for us?' I asked.

'Not bad, slight off-to-leg slope from the pavilion end.'

'Got any bowlers who can use it?'

'We've a little leg-spinner I have hopes for.'

I winced, I hadn't properly inoculated my team against leg-spin. It could run through a prep-school batting line-up like cholera through a slum. 'Does he have a googly?'

'Ha-ha!' said Richard.

'Bastard . . . Talking of leg-spinners, what's happened to Tom Downey?' I asked.

'God knows,' said Richard. 'Last I heard he was living in a squat in Battersea'.

'And you're going to Trinity?'

'Yup. When term finishes here I'll be playing for Hampshire seconds. Next summer for the county proper, with any luck'.

'Still a cocky son of a bitch, then?'

Everyone has their time, I thought. You can meet people of thirty and know that when their hair is grey and their face lined, they will look wonderfully at their best. That professor for one, Donald Trefusis. He must have looked ridiculous as a teenager, but now he had come into his own. Others, whose proper age was twenty-five, grew old grotesquely, their baldness and thickening waistlines an affront to what they once were. There were men like that on the staff at Chartham, fifty or sixty years old, but whose true characters were only discernible in hints of some former passion and vigour that would come out when they were excited. The headmaster, on the other hand, was a pompous forty-one, waiting to ripen into a delicious sixty-five. What my own proper age was, I had no idea. Sometimes I felt I had left myself behind at school, at other times I thought I would be at my best in tubby and contented middle-age. But Richard . . . Richard I thought had little time between now and thirty-five in which to be glorious. Would I still be prepared to sacrifice all the other years of my life in exchange for ten years of first-class cricketing, I wondered? Travelling the world, hero-worshipped, adored, discussed, known by all cricket-lovers everywhere? Of course I would. Of bloody course I bloody would.

'I think we'll bat first, sir,' the Narborough Captain announced after winning the toss.

'That's it, Malthouse,' said Richard. 'Knock 'em up and bowl 'em out.'

'Trust me to lose the toss,' said Hooper. 'Sorry, sir.'

'Don't be a dafty-trousers,' I said. 'It's a good wicket to bat second on, it'll dry out all through the afternoon.'

I threw the ball to Rudder, Chartham's opening bowler, before taking my position at the stumps. 'Remember, Simon,' I said, 'straight and on a length, that's all you have to do.'

'Yes, sir,' said Rudder, swallowing.

The ground was in a kind of valley, with the looming Gothic of Narborough Hall on one rise and the church and village of Narborough on another. The pavilion was whitewashed and thatched, the weather perfect, only the faintest of breezes luffing the fielders' shirtsleeves. The grim seriousness of the children preparing to play, the detached amusement of Richard at square leg, the church clock chiming mid-day, the circles of fine gang-mown cuttings in the outfield, the sun winking off the roller by the sight-screen, the distant clatter of spiked shoes on the pavilion concrete, the open blue of the wide Norfolk sky, the six pebbles in the hand of my outstretched arm, this whole monstrous illusion froze, while to me the world seemed to hold its breath, as if uncertain that such a picture could last. This fantasy of England that old men took with them to their death-beds, this England without factories or sewers or council houses, this England of leather and wood and flannel, this England circumscribed by a white boundary and rules that said that each team shall field eleven men and that each man shall bat, this England of shooting-sticks, weather-vanes and rectory teas, it was like Richard's talent, I thought, a vision glimpsed for a second in an adolescent dream, then dispersed like steam into the real atmosphere of traffic-jams, serial murderers, prime ministers and vice. But its spectral haze was sharper and clearer than the glare of the everyday and, against all evidence, was taken to be the only reality, its vapour trapped and distilled in the mind, its images, scents and textures bottled and laid down against the long, lonely melancholy of adulthood.

I brought down my arm. 'Play!'

Rudder bowled a ball of full length and the batsman swept his bat elegantly forward in defence. But the ball had already gone through him and Rice the wicket keeper was leaping in glee. The batsman looked round in disbelief to see his off-stump lying on the ground. The poor boy returned to the pavilion shaking his head, as if Rudder had been guilty of some appalling social blunder. There was a light spatter of applause from the boundary. The school were in lessons and wouldn't be watching until after lunch.

I tossed a pebble into my right hand and smiled across at Richard.

'I got him, sir!' said Rudder, polishing the ball against his leg. 'I bloody got him. Golden bloody duck.'

'You beat him for pace, old love,' I said, drawing him aside. 'The next batsman will be scared. Bowl him two very quick ones just outside the line of off-stump and then a slower ball on middle, but disguise it.'

'All right, sir.'

I wondered if it was a breach of etiquette for an umpire to coach during play. But then I saw Richard, who had been replacing the bails at the other end, whispering urgently to the in-coming number three. Very well, then, we would fight it out between us, like First World War Generals.

Rudder did as he was told for the first two balls, letting them fly at the new batsman, who played and missed at the first and left the second alone. He came thundering up for the third ball, grunting and stamping like a buffalo. The batsman quaked.

'Subtle disguise I don't think,' I thought to myself.

The ball was let go of early and seemed to float in at half the speed. The batsman had nearly completed his defensive stroke by the time it got to him; as a result the ball was sent gently back to Rudder, who threw it up in the air with a yell of triumph.

'Caught and bowled! And hast thou slain the number three? Come to my arms, my beamish boy. Two for none, oh frabjous day, calloo callay!' I chortled in my joy.

Richard was furious at lunch. His side had been bowled out for fourteen runs. He couldn't believe it.

'I'll kill them!' he said. 'I'll castrate them and hang their scrotums from the scoreboard.'

'Don't worry,' I said. 'We'll probably be all out for ten.'

'I'm going to replace the whole team with boys from the scholarship Sixth. At least they'll have some brains. What good is ball sense without common sense? I mean, trying to square-cut a straight half-volley! It makes me want to throw up.'

I was sure that I wouldn't have sulked quite as gracelessly if it had been my side that had been dismissed for fourteen, but I forebore to comment.

'Look,' said Richard. 'If you do cream us straight after lunch, how would you feel about making it a two-innings match?'

'Well . . .'

'It'll go down as your victory of course, but we do need the practice.'

'All right,' I said. 'I'll check with my team first.'

Hooper was doubtful. 'We've never played two innings before, sir. What happens when we pass their first score?'

'We make as many runs as possible before we're all out.'

'Sir, suppose they can't get us all out?'

'That's when you have to declare, dear. Make sure you judge it so that there's time to put them in again, bowl them out and then pass their total before stumps. We don't want a draw.'

'When are stumps?'

'Narborough's Mr Waters and I agreed on seven o'clock. I'll have to ring the school and check with the headmaster. You'll all be late for bed of course, but it'll all be the most super-duper fun.'

The whole school turned out to watch after lunch. As I had feared, Narborough's leg-spinner, Ellis, completely baffled my boys. Once they had got used to the ball bouncing and spinning one way, he would send down top-spin and undetectable googlies that made the ball fly off to the waiting close field. We were all out for thirty-nine after an hour and a half of tortured embarrassment. Richard looked very smug as Narborough prepared for their second innings.

'We're only twenty-five ahead,' I said.

'That's all right, isn't it, sir?' said Rudder. 'If we get them out for fourteen again we'll have won by an innings and eleven runs.'

'If.'

The Narborough openers stalked to the wicket looking determined and confident. They were playing in front of their home crowd now and had experienced the satisfaction of seeing the Chartham team writhe.

Rudder's first ball was a wide. I signalled it, with raised eyebrows.

'Sorry, sir,' said Rudder with a grin.

His next ball was driven to the mid-off boundary, the next was hooked for six. The fourth, a no-ball, was late-cut for two which became six after four overthrows had been added. The next two were both glanced for four. Rudder turned to me to collect his sweater.

'Two more balls yet, Simon'.

'Sir?'

'There was a wide and a no-ball in there. Two more balls.'

'Oh. Yes, sir. I forgot.'

The next two were each smacked for four over Rudder's head.

'What's going wrong, sir?'

'What's going wrong is you're not bowling properly. Line and length, darling, line and length.'

For the next two hours the opening pair batted freely and fiercely, putting on 174, until one of the batsmen, the same man Rudder had clean bowled first ball of the morning, retired to let some of his friends enjoy the slaughter.

Richard's merriment was unbearable over tea. 'Well that's a bit more like it,' he said. 'I was beginning to get worried this morning.'

'Dear old friend of my youth,' I said. 'I'm afraid you've discovered our principal weakness.'

'What, you can't bowl you mean?'

'No, no. Sympathy. My boys were simply devastated by your glumness at lunch, so we decided to cheer you up by letting you have some batting practice. I take it you're declaring over tea?'

'You bet. Have you out of here, tail between your legs, by half-past five.'

'Is that a promise?' said a voice behind us. It was Professor Trefusis.

'Certainly, sir,' said Richard.

The Professor looked at me. 'What do you think?' he asked.

'Well, let me see . . . two hundred and thirty-nine to make before seven. I think we can do it all right, if we don't panic.'

'Ellis isn't tired, you know,' said Richard. 'He can bowl for hours at a stretch.'

'My boys were beginning to read him by the end,' I said. 'We can do it.'

'I have just placed a bet with my nephew Philip,' said Trefusis. 'Two hundred pounds on Chartham to win at odds of five to one against.'

'What?' I said. 'I mean . . . what?'

'I liked your entrance papers, most amusing. I don't see how you can fail.'

'Well,' said Richard as Trefusis ambled away. 'What a bloody idiot.'

'Oh, I don't know,' I said, popping a sandwich into my mouth. 'Smart investment if you ask me'.

'Right,' I said. 'There's a man out there who is so sure, based on the evidence of what he's seen, that you can do it, that he has bet two hundred pounds that you will blow these bastards out of the water.'

They were padding up in the pavilion, forlorn but brave, like Christians preparing for an away match against the Lions.

'But Ellis, sir!' said Hooper. 'He's impossible.'

'That's a trough of piss. You step up to him and you cart him all over the park, is what you do. Just don't get pushed against your stumps. Aim for the close-in fielders. If you miss the ball you might manage to belt them with your bat on the follow-through.'

'Isn't that a bit unsporting, sir?'

'Arseholes. Whistle, hum, look unconcerned, look bored. When he's ready to bowl, you step forward and say you're not ready. Disturb his rhythm, demonstrate contempt. Don't forget, I'm out there, and he'll want to bowl from my end because of the slope.'

'You won't *cheat* will you, sir?'

'Cheat? Good heavens. This is an amateur cricket match amongst leading prep schools, I'm an Englishman and a schoolmaster supposedly setting an example to his young charges. We are playing the most artistic and beautiful game man ever devised. Of course I'll cheat. Now, give me my robe, put on my crown; I have immortal longings in me.'

Out in the middle, little Ellis took the ball and flipped it from hand to hand, with the disturbing competence of a born spinner of the ball.

I patted his head.

'Good luck, little chap,' I said. 'Don't get upset if they punish you a bit. It's only a game, eh?'

Ellis looked puzzled. 'Yes, sir.'

A sporting round of applause from the Narborough boys welcomed Chartham's opening pair to the wicket.

'Here they come now. They're both rather savage

hitters of the ball, I'm afraid. But if you don't lose your head you should be able to cut it down to ten or so an over. A word of advice, though. Try and do something about disguising that googly of yours a bit better . . . sticks out like a sore thumb.'

Ellis tweaked the ball out of the side of his hand uncertainly.

'Thank you, sir.'

'All right. Here we go. Don't be nervous.'

Frowde and Colville, the openers, had certainly taken my game-plan literally. They surveyed the field with lofty disdain and smiled faint patronising smiles at the short-leg and silly point crowded around them, nicely blending admiration for their physical courage with doubt for their mental capacity. They were welcome to stand there and be cut in two, but they had been warned.

'Play!' I commanded.

Ellis stepped forward. Frowde at the other end threw up a hand and bent to do up his shoelaces. 'Sorry!' he called. 'Won't be a sec.'

Ellis turned back to his mark and waited.

'All right, Frowde?' I asked.

'Fine thank you, sir. Just don't want to get tangled up when I start running.'

'Quite so.' I dropped my arm. 'Play!!' I boomed.

Ellis bowled a full-toss which Frowde hooked straight over the boundary. The short-leg fielder glared at Ellis. The ball had nearly decapitated him.

I signalled a four to the scorer.

'It was a six,' said Richard at square leg.

'Sorry?'

'It was a six!'

'Are you sure?'

'Of course I'm sure! It went clean over.'

'Well if you're sure,' I said, signalling a six. 'I didn't want to give ourselves two extra runs. That was a six, scorer!' I yelled, just as Ellis next to me was catching the return from deep mid-wicket. The blast in his ear made him drop the ball. I picked it up for him.

'Try and get them to bounce on the ground first,' I said helpfully. 'That way it's harder for the batsman to hit quite so far.'

Ellis's second was a long-hop square-cut for four.

'You see?' I said. 'That's two fewer already.'

The next was on a good length and driven straight to close extra-cover.

'There might be a couple here,' shouted Frowde to his partner.

'Genius,' I thought, as they ran one run after the extra-cover fielder fumbled the ball in his amazement at the possibility that anyone was going to run at all.

Ellis was made of stout stuff. His next ball was an excellent leg-break that nearly had Colville stumped.

I walked forward and patted the pitch with my foot. 'You must watch your feet after you've bowled,' I told him. 'You're not allowed to run on in the area between the two wickets. It kicks up rough stuff and helps the bowler at the other end.'

Little Ellis was aghast at the possibility that I might

have thought he had been trying to cheat. 'I'm very sorry, sir,' he said. 'I didn't mean . . .'

'Of course you didn't, my dear fellow. That was just a warning, that's all. I'm sure it won't happen again.'

Ellis bowled the next ball from so wide of the stumps that it glanced straight across Colville for four byes.

He was taken off after three more catastrophic overs and retired to long-on, blinking back tears and fending off the jeers of his home supporters on the boundary.

'Cricket,' I thought. 'It's so character-building.'

After the collapse of Ellis the outcome was never really in doubt. The fast man at the other end was competent but soon exhausted. Weirder and wilder alternatives were tried: boys who dropped slow balls from a great height, boys with violent actions like windmills that produced gentle long-hops, boys who bowled balls that bounced twice before reaching the middle of the pitch; but to no avail. The openers put on a stand of 112 and the fourth-wicket partnership of Rice and Hooper scored the final runs as the Narborough church clock struck six.

I watched it all with raised eyebrows and an impartial smile. Richard boiled and seethed and glared, glancing miserably from time to time at the stony figure of his headmaster, who sat perched on a shooting-stick next to Professor Trefusis.

'An instructive match,' I said as we pulled up the stumps. 'I thought we were in real trouble at one stage.'

'I can't understand what the hell went wrong with Ellis,' said Richard. 'I really thought he was the most gifted cricketer in the school. A county prospect even.'

'He's young yet. Temperament is the problem there, I fancy. I tried to calm him down and encourage him to get on with his natural game, but he was a bit overawed. Don't give up on him, he's learnt a lot today.'

'He'll have learnt a bloody sight more after I'm through with him.'

The Narborough team, hot and limp with exertion and defeat, saw us off in the driveway. Richard stood with us, pulling glumly at a can of beer.

'Three cheers for Chartham Park,' called Malthouse, their Captain, raising his arm with an attempt at casual gallantry. 'Hip-ip.'

'Ray!' murmured Narborough.

'Hip-ip.'

'Ray!'

'Hip-ip.'

'Ray.'

'Three cheers for Narborough Hall,' shouted a flushed and triumphant Hooper, punching the air. 'Hip-hip!'

'Hooray!' bellowed Chartham.

'Hip-Hip-Hip!'

'Hooray!'

'Hip-Hip-Hip-Hip!'

'HOORAY!'

'Goodbye then Richard. See you for the return match.'

'We'll pulverise you.'

'Of course you will.'

Trefusis stepped forward.

'Well young man, you've earned me a thousand pounds. Here's two hundred, my original stake.'

'Oh really,'I said, 'I couldn't.'

'Of course you could.' He pushed a bundle of notes at me. 'Tremendous display.'

'Yes, they're not a bad bunch, are they?' I looked on affectionately as my team climbed into the minibus.

'No, no, no. You!'

'Professor?'

'I knew that the man who wrote those artfully disguised second-hand essays, who disgorged such specious and ill-thought-out nonsense with such persuasive and brilliant flair wouldn't let me down. You've clearly a genius for deceit and chicanery. I look forward to seeing you next term.'

Tom Downey and I watched gloomily from our box as Richard trudged back to the pavilion. 'Don't think he'll be on for dinner tonight,' said Tom.

'Poor sod,' I said. 'Just imagine what the papers are going to say tomorrow.'

'Yeah.'

A waitress came forward and thrust a napkin at Tom. 'I'm ever so sorry . . . If you could . . .'

'What's your name darling?'

I still marvelled at Tom's spurious cockney vowels and the unassailable position he still held after ten years of rock stardom. Other fashions had come and gone but Tom Downey would always be . . . well, cool.

As if reading my thoughts, he tilted his sunglasses down onto the bridge of his nose and peered at me over them.

'It's a livin',' he said.

'A multi-million-pound living,' I said.

'You don't do too bad yourself.'

'No,' I said. 'I suppose I don't. I've been very lucky.'

The familiar voice of an old Yorkshire and England player drifted across from a neighbouring box. 'I mean absolutely *pathetic*. It's as if Waters doesn't know the first principles of the game.'

'He's talented, though,' said his companion. 'Lovely stylist.'

'Oh, he can *play*, I'll grant you. But frankly . . .'

Desultory and cynical cheers greeted the next batsman. The Lord's crowd were disappointed and embarrassed by their side. Australia was walloping us. The droop of Richard's shoulders as he had returned, Captain of England, to the most famous pavilion in the world, bowled out for five, had said it all.

'He's only got another three years in him, of course,' said the Yorkshireman gleefully.

I looked at Tom and sighed.

'Yes,' I said, 'I've been lucky. Bloody, bloody lucky.'

The First Saturday in May

J.L. CARR

IN THE PRE-WAR Spring of 1936 I removed from Hampshire, where I had been playing village cricket with Curdridge (annual subscription five shillings and all found) and took a job in Birmingham.I joined Aston Unity, whose professional then was Eric Cooper, who had come down from Lancashire and later played for Worcestershire. Unity was a rather grand no-nonsense club playing in the Birmingham & District League against sides like Walsall (professional: A.P. Freeman) and Smethwick (Sydney Barnes). Its subscription was twenty-five shillings, and one was expected to provide oneself with a complete set of paraphernalia (except wickets and bails) and 'a respectable bag' to carry it around in.

For my first game I was picked, quite properly, for the 3rd XI, whose opening fixture was away against

Bridgnorth 1st team. Only the captain owned a car and he crammed six into it. The rest of us were detailed to make our way by rail and, about eleven in the morning, we met at Snow Hill station. A Great Western steam locomotive backed two or three carriages down the long gloomy platform and off we jogged. Smethwick ... Quarry Bank ... Stourbridge ... Hagley ... Blakedown ... we stopped at all of them.

But here's *noblesse oblige* for you. Robert Gardner, the club's Hon. Sec., travelled along with us. The Hon. Sec.! His aura transformed an expedition of outcasts into a cabal – sharers of the inner counsels of the First XI.

It is a long time ago. But I remember that it was very hot when we got out at Kidderminster to lug our bags across the platform and into an empty compartment of a second train. Then as we set off westward once more (Oldington Halt ... Devil's Spittlend Halt) we jerked up the leather straps to let down both windows and, now clear of the Black Country, let in country sounds and smells.

I recall peering down from an embankment at Wribbenhall because one of our party claimed that an uncle there had told him very odd things happened on Saturday nights, things he wouldn't like talking about, terrible things. 'But it's different over the bridge in Bewdley,' he added. 'Bewdley is really elegant. Stanley Baldwin lives just up the road from Bewdley.'

'Thank God for Stanley Baldwin. Solid chap!' the Hon. Sec. said. 'Whatever that Charlie Chaplin over in Germany is up to, you can rely on Stanley Baldwin. Take my word for it. Smokes Three Nuns, too . . .' (lighting his pipe).

Then we went north for a half-mile to cross the river into the Wyre Forest. As we turned westward into higher country the locomotive was labouring; we were making a lot of smoke. At the first halt the stationmaster (doubling as porter and ticket-collector) ranged the platform calling 'Far Forest! Far Forest!' It had a despairing sound. No-one got out, no-one got in. As we moved off I saw him looking reproachfully after us. Even then, when young Beeching was still in his first long trousers and wrestling with his school-certif, *that* line was doomed.

We wandered along; conversation turned inevitably and acrimoniously to that topic most favoured by all 3rd XIs: a hanging judgement of 2nd and 1st XIs. 'That's enough of that,' the Hon. Sec. said gruffly, 'you don't know all the ins and outs of it.'

We crawled past Cleobury Mortimer Junction and somewhere near Nineveh I heard my first cuckoo. The sun still shone: it was a perfect day for cricket. As we halted at Neen Sollers someone remarked that we seemed to have been travelling for a long time, and Bob Gardner fished into a waistcoat pocket and examined his watch.

Then, at Tenbury Wells, he poked out his head and called to a porter, 'How much further to Bridgnorth?' I didn't catch the answer but it must have shaken him. 'We've got to get out,' he told us. 'We're on the wrong line: this one goes to Ludlow. We should have changed at Bewdley.'

So, shamefaced, we hung about the little station's entrance and watched him walk fiercely into the town. The stationmaster had no comfortable news. Bridgnorth lay twenty miles to the north-east. No, there was no train service in that directiion. We must travel back to Wribbenhall and change onto the Shrewsbury line. He expected that our friend must have gone to see his son-in-law who owned a taxi, so he would stretch a point and not charge us excess fare for our journey in the wrong direction.

The Secretary reported that he'd found a hired car and that the chap would take the five of us for fifty shillings. This was financial disaster of the first order: I was only earning £16 a month and my lodgings were expensive. There was mutiny in the air until we were reminded of what our late headmasters might have expected of us, what the club would expect of us, and what he, the Hon. Sec., *did* expect of us. Gloomily, we handed over our ten-bob notes.

The car turned up. 'Them bags,' its proprietor complained, 'they take up the same room near enough as five chaps.' We forked out an extra half-crown apiece. It was 2.30 p.m. by the station clock; twenty miles away the opening batsmen of one side or the other would be walking out to the wickets.

Fifty years later I still remember that desperate journey. Not in exact detail, of course – that would be asking too much. But I recall that Salopian roads are

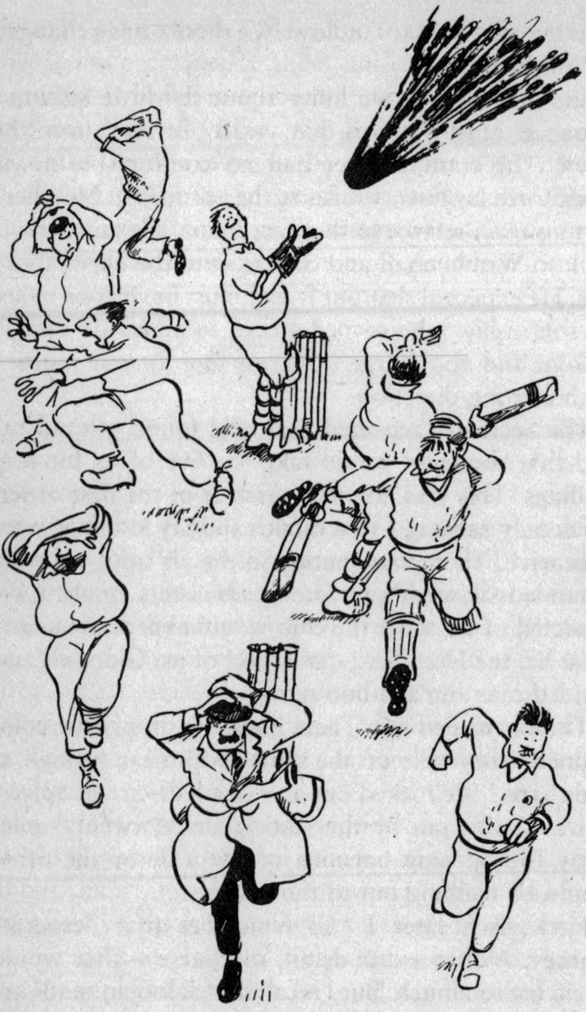

notable wanderers. To our left, Titterston Clee heaved up sharply from rising fields. Then there was Hope Bagot, Earl's Ditton, Lubberland, Hardwick Forge. Soon we turned north-east under the long ridge of Brown Clee till it ended on the ancient camp of Abdon Burf. Now and then, by some lonely hillside farm, wild cherry trees were in bloom. This was A.E. Housman country, and a line or two learnt at school up in Yorkshire came back to mind:

On the idle hill of summer,
Sleepy with the flow of streams . . .

And, eventually, we reached Bridgnorth Cricket Club's ground. Four men were out, the score was derisory. Numbers five and six, batting as men bemused, were holding out like a desert garrison awaiting a relief column. The captain seemed to be on the verge of a nervous breakdown. Making his lame excuses, the Club Secretary seemed to have shrunk to the same size as the rest of us. We were bustled into our gear and, one after another, flung into the breach.

I can't remember the final total. Certainly it was no more than a few beyond a hundred. Well, it was a long time ago.

In fact, my one abiding memory of the match itself is of a Bridgnorth opening batsman. (I should like to know his name.) He was a stocky, strong man, and he relentlessly flogged our bowling. Perhaps he was punishing not only us but Aston Unity, even Birmingham itself, for sending a Third XI. I was fielding long-on and third-man, picketing the Saturday morning cattle-mart boundary. Perhaps that batsman was a farmer, perhaps an auctioneer. Anyway, time after time the ball ended up amongst that morning's occupants' misadventures, and had to be dredged from animal ordure, sludge and worse. Their skipper kept us in the field and me in and out of the cattle-mart until his man had made a century. Then they scornfully declared.

In the cool of the evening, and feeling sorry for ourselves, the five of us traipsed wearily down through the town to the railway station. There things began to look up: an amiable middle-aged woman kept open the platform refreshment room until the down train from Shrewsbury picked us up. Then, first in the dusk and then in the darkness, we travelled south down the Severn's valley.

The forest was to our right now, the river to our left. At Hampton Loade it was so still that I heard water slipping by in the darkness. We must have been the last train at Highley, because a porter followed along the platform putting out oil lamps. No-one spoke. I think we knew that, for one reason or another, it had been a day we should remember.

At Arley Ferry someone on the further bank swung a lamp and, nearer us amongst trees, a girl's call answered. Soon a line of lights was reflected in the river. The Club Secretary heartlessly broke this enchantment. 'Bewdley', he said. 'This is where we should have changed trains on the way out.'

Well, we shall not make that mistake again.

On the idle hill of summer,
Sleepy with the flow of streams,
Far I hear the steady drummer,
Drumming like a noise in dreams . . .

But that afternoon, I hadn't remembered, hadn't heard, those last two lines. At least two of us would die in fixtures even then tentatively arranged for our careless generation.

And now, those charmingly inconsequential railways have been found out by accountants, so that no-one ever again will call 'Far Forest! Far Forest!' Nor, at Tenbury Wells, ask how far it is to anywhere. And I am left remembering the heat of the day, the burden of fielding ankle-deep in Bridgnorth's cattle-mart, snow storms of hillside blossom. And wondering if a change of trains or, for that matter, a change of anything, really is for the better.

Roundhead Cricket

EDWARD PEARCE

THE PLEASURE OF cricket is different in kind from the pleasure of all other sports. Better than most athletic undertakings it is generous to the unathletic. Considering how badly the game can be played it is rather like charity in the bible: it suffereth long and is kind.

The game can exist at different levels in a way which is frankly pointless in all the running and jumping activities. There a measured statistical objective exists and is either approached, in which case the outing is relevant, or not, in which case it isn't. Cricket, by contrast, can be a source of intense pleasure both at the David Gower level of delicate and fascinating grace or miles below among the most clumping and experimental of village green or knock-up sides.

You can have the deadly competitive extension of war-by-other-means, or you may enjoy Tillingfold cricket, the sort celebrated by Hugh de Selincourt in his famous book, *The Cricket Match*. At Tillingfold there is pleasure in victory and every sporting excitement but also a social feeling, friendly acquaintance with the other side, the pleasure of the morning in town before the match, the pleasure of Mr MacDonald the bat carrier and his special little dinner afterwards. You could do a Marxist analysis of *The Cricket Match* and its bourgeois contentment and very funny it would be. A good part of a very decent English life resides in that sort of happy cricket.

However, the game also benefits from its length and the element of strategy which leaves it, like chess, full of options and alternative moves. The time-out, that slightly improbably episode we have grown familiar with through the televising of American football, is a continual presence, a running consultation; in cricket indeed at its most parodistic our game can look like one continuous time-out. To paraphrase Fernand Braudel, it is *le jeu de la longue durée*, cricket as Mahler would have played it. (Latterly, if we are into musical comparisons, English cricket has been at the level of Sterndale Bennett on a bad day.)

For cricket is assuredly a game of strategy, a form of bloodless war-game. The best demonstration of this strategic (and tactical) cricket came, not in Test matches, needle matches with blunt needles even in the days when we sometimes won one, but in old-fashioned Roses cricket. The object became not victory, a flashy, 'over-the-top' objective, but 'seeing off t'other lot'.

I shall not forget coming home one day from school

to be motioned to silence by my father who was crouched over the radio. It had been a dreadful match against Yorkshire, dreadful in the only sense that mattered: they were winning. And my father carried (and passed on) the prejudices of Oldham into exile. But the message that afternoon was one of anxious delight. 'Washbrook and the wicket-keeper are still there.' The fact that they must have scored about thirty in three hours was neither here nor there: Cyril Washbrook and Alan Wilson were preventing defeat, as indeed by stumps they had finally succeeded in doing.

Because the conflict mattered across the Pennines, followers of the game were not interested in the trivial theatricals of boundary-bashing Sunday television cricket and had distinctly marginalised their otherwise sharp regard for strokeplay. They were focussed upon the contest and would applaud whatever resolute dead hand of negation would settle it *their* way.

Incidentally, that odd acrimony between counties owes nothing to the floral rhetoric of fifteenth-century late-feudal gangsters. There was then, may still be, an intense feeling in the North that respectively Lancastrians were soft-headed urban yokels, too close to Ireland and generally feckless, open-mouthed, slow-spoken Formby clones/generous, open-hearted models of gentle good nature, spiked with murmured ironies; and that Yorkshiremen were hard-faced, hard-hearted ha'penny-clutchers, descendants of the more psychopathic stray Vikings, with all the charity of a bunch of knuckles/strong, self-sufficient, iron-spirited, plain-spoken heroes, every man half iron-puddler, half alderman in good standing.

Given such preconceptions, the game played at Sheffield, Leeds and Manchester had no room for such wicket-chancing, gay blade fal-diddle as may lightly pass across eighty overs of a Sunday on camera between flippant Surrey and laid-back Northamptonshire. If the context is civilised enough a little hatred adds piquancy. The organisers of cricket festivals, not often imaginative men, are given to calling their scratch sides things like 'Lady Brassborough's Cavaliers'. In Lancashire and Yorkshire, where a leg-glance is an imputation of homosexuality, lace is rarely worn at the throat and long curls are at a discount, where ruffles receive knowing looks, we are into that least pronounced-upon aspect of the game, 'Roundhead Cricket'.

Such local particularism is all very foolish and occasionally not altogether nice, witness Yorkshire's obdurate Leninism, the cricket-in-one-county policy which, at one stage, degenerated into a discreet piece of black exclusion. But the tight Northern approach did lead to an intelligent, long-sighted understanding of the game. The notorious cry of anguish at a four struck by one's own side, 'Nay, lad, tek it steady', is in contrast with the demand for high-scoring, lightly entertaining play, a demand which grows petulant if not rewarded. Such supporters drink lager and make last-night-of-the-proms noises. Unlike such indulgence in the pleasure principle, the old Northern game acknowledges the war-game and long strategy aspects of cricket, positively delighting in a hard-tack diet of attrition. I respect that outlook but I should hate to have to watch it if anyone other than Lancashire were involved. I should urge upon a mere Warwickshire batsman a degree of abandon and excess which would outrage me at Old Trafford.

At the heart of England's failure, conspicuously in 1989 but just to say noticeably over many years now, lie several things. One is a failure to teach cricket in schools, born partly of a foolish teacher-training college hostility to 'a hierarchical-competitive ethos', sociologist's thinking quite amazing to the steady Labour voters of the Northern grounds.

Then too there have been some unimaginably foolish and inadequate old fools at the top of the game. Peter May, with his incoherence, terror of communication, random decisions and a wavering eptitude totally at odds with his own immaculate game, managed to look like Jim Prior presiding over the end of the world. Ted Dexter of the fast cars and barking manner, a sort of Max Hastings of the pavilion, is so far just looking like another First World War general.

But the decline or loss of chic of the dark, bitter, stalking Northern game is another factor. With the honourable exception of Robin Smith, a South African, and, intermittently, of Jack Russell, there is nobody able to do a Cyril Washbrook. The saviour of Lancashire also, when recalled at the very end of a great career, walked all day to a memorable unscheduled 98 in a Test when all around were doing what they usually do. We are short of obduracy during collapse.

Incidentally and by way of parenthesis, in the relations of Lord's and the North, one notices without pleasure that the committee is happiest with the educated classes. Mike Atherton is a talent who may come to something or not. What assuredly he is not is a tested, seasoned, fully in-form player who has found his stride. So far Atherton is a few strokes, a university degree and a lot of talk. That from a Lancashire containing the eligible Mendis, Fairbrother and Fowler, indeed Watkinson, the committee should choose a young gentleman who in terms of his place in the table of averages is ninety-something, speaks oceans about the standing of young gentlemen. The England committee seem to take a remarkably exalted view of a BA from Durham.

Yet this choice is nowhere challenged in the press. One recalls without pleasure the embarrassing copy of John Thicknesse in 1988, twisting a humble flat cap in his honest workman's hands as he tried to find words adequate to praise the glories of Christopher Cowdrey, 102nd in those averages if I remember rightly, but May's godson, and chosen, disastrously, as captain. The social reverence of a large part of the press can be counted on. Though it can also be trusted to savage real talent when they have it, witness the simple hatred expended upon David Gower, a moderate captain of a weak side but also the most perfect batting stylist of his generation. He was then in deference to these tranting oafs insanely omitted from the doomed touring side. (They would have been annoyed at Gower's delicate style at Bramall Lane if he had been a Yorkshireman – 'tekkin too many risks' – but they would have noticed and admired it!)

It seems to me that at the moment in England we have the worst of the options. We have cavaliers (or Tory wets) in the committee room, liquorice allsorts in the team and foreign tanks on the ground. We need many things to get the game right: a change of heart in the state schools or a great throwing open of the gates guarding their quality coaching by the public schools, something which really should be pursued.

We also need access to the first-class league. This has stayed unaltered for 69 years since Glamorgan's accession. Durham come close to meeting the requirements; but what is wrong with double-county applications, allowing wider catchments and resources? Northants playing in Hertfordshire and Bedfordshire already do this, so why not, say, Norfolk-and-Suffolk, Shropshire-and-Staffordshire? Perhaps we might thus find a cricketing Wimbledon, not to mention a Vinny Jones, which would upset the Long Room. On second thoughts, no, we *don't* want a Vinny Jones.

But whatever reforms we may adopt we have to be clear what the objective is. If cricket is to be enjoyed, sweetly, socially and with defeat tearing no heartstrings, then we stop playing the hard games. We give up Australia and the West Indies for Lent and think very hard about Pakistan.

THE CROMWELL ENCLOSURE
T'SCORING RATE'S GONE UP TO 3 AN HOUR. I HATE THESE SUNDAY BASHES!

If we want to avoid both such withdrawal and endemic defeat, we must dress in the basin helmets of Cromwell's good russet-coated captain that knows what he fights for and loves what he knows. We have, in fact, to adapt to the Roundhead cricket of the old Northern game. Which course, let us be clear, involves working up feelings of antipathy so deep that internationally expressed they might lead to exchanges of notes and withdrawals of legations. Such an approach would also involve playing for a draw from the first ball and educating a crowd raised on lollipops to the strategic glories of a three-hour fifty.

It will seem to many people that for us to stop losing, cricket will have to matter more than cricket can matter and that a graceful retreat towards the world of Tillingfold, towards, that is, a TV commercial shot in soft focus, is our best way out of things. There is this small thought: Australia, weighed down with social resentment, not only hates us more than we absently dislike them. For Australia is a separate British social class as well as another country. It is a spilt proletariat with an outback. Accordingly not only do Australians play the sport with an intensity which Bramall Lane would understand, though nobody can hold a candle to the Australian nation for idle, unproductive, parasitic approach to the economy; also, such residuum of puritanism as they may have is solidly invested in 'cruck-ett'.

Something of the grace of this singularity of purpose was expressed in an instructive small episode by Mr

Allan Border. A polite, tentative and anxious citizen approached him with a gentle request for a signature. 'Fuck off', said Mr Border.

That is the winning spirit, if not quite as Cromwell would have expressed it. It is the way of neither Tillingfold *nor* Cyril Washbrook. Long contemplation of Mr Border, for all his skill, courage and control of the team, makes inept defeat seem perfectly acceptable. On the other hand perhaps we really could get to hate Australia.

Cricket, Lovely Cricket

FREDERIC RAPHAEL

SIGMUND FREUD ONCE observed that the reason that money failed to make people happy was that its accumulation did not correspond to any childhood wish. It may be assumed that no inventory of his dreams would disclose an unsatisfied desire to play first-class cricket. A Viennese 'witch doctor' (Vladimir Nabokov's unflattering description of the founder of psycho-analysis) might be at a loss to understand the persistence of such reveries in the sub-conscious of those born under other skies. My own childhood had – so to say – two innings. Until I was eight years old, I was promised (by my German-born grandfather) that my national game was baseball. Max Mauser had transferred his patriotism from Germany to the USA before the Great War, at the age of fourteen, when he travelled alone from Bad Kreuznach to New

York. He achieved neither fame nor fortune, but he was, unlike Arthur Miller's salesman, Willie Loman, not only liked but *well* liked. He was popular even with Kansas City mobsters who were known as 'The Prendergast Gang'. On one occasion he was offered the job of food inspector; he declined selection with moral prudence. Max never played American games, but he was eager that I should; hence Babe Ruth was the first batsman ('batter' was the Yankee term) to whose (home-)run-hitting talents I was alerted.

We came to England in 1938, as the result of an administrative decision in the multi-national corporation which employed my father (who had kept wicket for the Nomads, in *glass* glasses, after coming down from Oxford). It was, I need hardly remind those of my generation, the summer in which Hutton broke the record for a Test-match innings against Australia. Bill Edrich made a duck in the same innings; Joe Hardstaff made a scarcely-remembered century to add to Hutton's 364 n.o. in fattening the England total to, if memory serves, 903 for seven. Those who have taken a keen interest in my cricketing career will know that the war years interrupted it as severely, though not as gloriously, as that of Edrich W.J., who passed the years between his ignominy at the Oval and his apotheosis in the Middlesex (and England) season of 1947 winning decorated glory in the Air Force.

Freud would, I suppose, sigh indulgently at the clarity with which I recall the cricketers of my early and middle adolescence. The long immaturity of the

English, their slowness to adapt to the reality principle, and to concede that it is time to put away childish things, may well find its ideal correlative in a green dream of unchanging days in which Compton and Edrich forever open the innings and, in the impossible time remaining, hit off the sixty-odd runs needed to defeat Leicestershire (wasn't it?) in thirty-five minutes or so. The screen of memory is golden with heroes who gave Middlesex the championship by such a margin that the county's later achievements seem like pale echoes. Can we ever look at a helmeted batsman, however understandably cowled against hurtled hostility, and not remember the incredulity with which Rex or John or Howard (how the voices burble together in the great blender of sentimental recall!) remarked 'And here comes Compton, *in a cap*'? Compton D.C.S., whose gallant dishevelment was so happy a contrast with his Brylcreemed image on London Transport billboards, was never intimidated by Lindwall or Miller, Davidson or Toshack (oh, those wickedly rearing cutters of his!), but Denis showed unusual deference to the sun before unleashing one of those unwise sweeps to leg which no sports master could endorse. (To this day I can never wholly respect anyone who spells his Denis with two n's.)

Why do the names of cricketers tend to bob to memory's surface in pairs? Who was the legendary figure who batted with Barlow in the poem which celebrated 'long ago'? He meant nothing to me, but Barnes goes with Morris in the litany of my boyhood as Hillard goes with Botting, who opened for Latin grammar when dead languages became my vocation (I was called to them, they never called to me). I never saw 'Patsy' Hendren and J.W. Hearn (did he wear an 'e' or not?), but I can hum along with songs in their praise.

Even bowlers came in the dual, so to say: some of us will never forget those 'little powers of mine/Ramadhin and Valentine', though I don't know who turned his arm over at the other end when Clarrie Grimmett or Kent's Doug Wright was working his wizardry (very expensive, Wright, D.V.P., but worth every penny and years ahead of his time, Rex Alston used to tell us, before handing back to John Arlott as Hassett prepared to take strike with a characteristic tug of that baggy green cap, and in came Doug with that kangaroo run of his . . .).

Opening batsmen had, of course, an option on prompt, as it were twin, veneration: Woodfull and Ponsford were, apparently, undentable until Lol broke their nerve and Woodfull's head, though He Never Meant To Do It. For me, the pair of Robertson and Brown were hardly less reliable. Jack played for England, though not as often as he might have, had he been able to resist the temptation to cut an early delivery, with an elegance that was typical of everything he did, into the hands of third slip. Robertson – if he could survive that single symptom of a reckless spirit – could make a hundred as handsomely as – and more economically than – the Famous Pair, Bill and Denis, whom he must have known the people in the Large

WHY DO I ALWAYS THINK OF
GREAT BOWLERS COMING
IN PAIRS ?

Mound Stand (2/6d extra) had really come to see. How can we judge what effect it had on Jack to know that the public knew that Bill was waiting, padded and tigerish on the players' balcony, for that first wicket to fall?

Jack's economy lay in his use of the enemy's energy in his own humiliation, not that he ever showed the smallest sign of relishing the frustration of those whose thunderbolts he sent, with a feathery touch, rattling with the force of their own propulsion against the pavilion pickets. When his touch, no less feathery, did not deviate the ball quite past the wicket keeper – when, in a word, he got himself caught – Jack walked like a gentleman. Some player, his middle name might have been Gunga-Din. When, on happier days, he got a hundred without removing his sweater (he did not like to *run*, though he made an art of walking) Jack acknowledged our applause by slowly removing his cap, the better to replace it.

'Sailor' Brown was his straight man. Where Jack made his seasonal two or three thousands, Brown – were his initials really S.M.? – was content with his thousand plus. He was a beefy man, with a rolling gait (matched by Jim Sims, who tweaked when Bill's rockets or Laurie Gray's steady pace failed to dislodge the visitors). Brown carried a hefty bat, but he was the dispensable pace-maker *par excellence*, whose departure was clapped with a mixture of condolence and delight, since we were about to see What We Had Really Come For.

But I must not strain your patience: not everyone,

for some reason, supports Middlesex. I fear I cannot reveal my even-handed respect for the opening pairs of other counties in those sunny days of Snoek and Whalemeat (who opened for the Ministry of Food), because I cannot remember their famous names. As for the England pair, in the era when teams were not picked but picked themselves, until senility obliged resignation, Hutton and Washbrook were, despite the latter's noble last performance (it made Sidney Carton's look a little flashy) never quite heroic: they sometimes succeeded, but they did not have the against-all-odds *réclame* which procures first-team selection in the Elysian Fields. I never saw Hobbs and Sutcliffe, though I was with them all the way, in retrospective spirit, when they opened on a sticky dog – in Melbourne, was it? – and stayed there till stumps on that inter-war tour Wally Hammond described in the book he published soon after the war.

Hammond's memoirs made as marked an impression as Somerset Maugham's *A Writer's Notebook*, which came into my hands at about the same time. To be both a published author *and* an England regular was, I can now frankly confess, the ambition which made even Charterhouse a place of optimistic dreams. As you know, the double achievement eluded me, but a man's reach can exceed his grasp. To how few is it given to bowl from both ends at the same time, so to say! Denis, of course – hardly a 'man' in the mundane sense – should have been a full soccer international in the days when his knee was reliable for The Arsenal, but the war was A Cruel Interruption, you will recall.

The fulfilment of A Unique Sporting Double was left to Watson (Sunderland and England *and* Leicestershire and England). Watson (oh what were his initials?) partnered Trevor Bailey at Lord's in that Day-Long Defiance Of Everything The Aussies Could Throw At Them. T.E. Bailey (Cambridge and Essex) crowned the term 'forward defensive' with all the allure once reserved for a hook for six. Since then, the One-Day Game (enter The Villain) has sanctioned recklessness, to the point, quite candidly, of near-immorality (see under Swinging Sixties), with all the spineless – not to say 'spinless' (see under Leg-Break, legendary, also Wright, D.V.P.) – consequences We All Deplore.

I still have my copy of Wally's memoirs (no offers will be accepted), but I cannot lay a hand on it in order to verify whether it was really called *Cricket is My Business*. So frank a mercenary confession seems implausible for a man who had turned amateur in order to captain his country, to crushing defeat, in the Australian tour of 1946-47, when Edrich, W.J. (later to become W.J. Edrich, though he never, for Certain Reasons, captained his country) bravely returned to Ashes cricket. His ribs a xylophone for the pitiless Aussie bumpers, he made seventeen (top score) on yet another sticky dog. It was only thirteen years since Jardine. That Gutsy Knock was, of course, A Portent Of Things To Come. The South Africans, who were still Welcome Guests in those days before Dr Malan and his sordid epigones, felt the full weight of Bill's recovered strength when he knocked them for six after six in his Year of Triumph.

But why rehash what is already sufficiently illuminated in the Halls of Cricketing Fame? You want – and I can understand your impatience – to hear more about me. Like Brigadier Gerard, I must defer to your curiosity and, despite the habit of modesty (P.B.H. May again leaves his mark), not disappoint your insistence.

I never played for any team of greater quality than Lockites, my Charterhouse house, whose apple-green 'square' – proof of having 'received houseteams' (or house colours) – is in my trophy drawer. Pundits may argue that I was equally honoured by brief selection for the East Bergholt village side.

Had my residential constancy been greater, I might have commanded a regular place at the beginning of the Sixties. There is wide agreement that my most memorable achievement in Essex was that innings of seven not out of which, primed with the right company and claret of the same year (1961), I can sometimes be tempted, on long summer evenings, into a never-too-long analysis. Vivid with locally colourful reminiscences of country pubs and rosy-cheeked Constable-countrymen, of fast bowlers who, after I had defied them for more than twenty minutes, went on to play for the County Second Eleven, my widely-solicited tales can send listeners home ready for dreamless sleep, if not already comatose. Ah, memory! Batted, gloved and (let us be candid) boxed, how patiently you sit in the pavilion of the past, waiting for a ghostly knock!

The circumstances of my premature retirement from Serious Competition at the age of not-quite-eighteen have intrigued researchers. The tale of the graceless schoolboy wicket-keeper whom I broke a long and dignified silence to accuse, with sorry accuracy, of having appealed for a catch when I had manifestly shouldered arms to a ball which clipped my pads, might, in an ideal world, have been expected to evoke a word of apology from the scoundrel, after all these unjust years. Imagine if Shakespeare had walked away from the Globe, and from play writing, after a foolish decision of the stage manager not to allow him to play the Second Murderer!

Since the publication elsewhere of the relevant facts, the guilty wicket keeper has indeed, in his fashion broken the silence of almost forty years. Like Senator McCarthy, I have his letter here in my hand. I could wish to report that a mature conscience had engendered remorse and that, despite worldly success and grand-paternity, my one-time school-fellow now felt that Apologies Were Due. As Neville Chamberlain more or less said, I have to tell you that no such communication has reached me. In fact, the letter I have received not only refrains from any *amende honorable*, but openly, impudently, threatens legal action if I ever mention Mickey's full name again. I cannot, as he well knows, and cynically assumes, risk the fate of Count Tolstoy, or the Lottery of the Libel

Courts, by revealing (or repeating) ALL, but you know, and I know, that Things Might Have Been Different. The cult of Success At All Costs has turned Our Game, if not the World Itself, into the moral morass which, alas, alas (as General de Gaulle so rightly said, twice), it certainly is today. If batsmen now rarely, if ever, 'walk', it is because of decisions like the one which Drove Me From The Game In Disgust. No, I wouldn't say 'bitter' exactly, Richie, more disillusioned.

If, to use the jargon of the VDU generation, I vanished from the public screen, in cricketing terms, after 1949 (my *annus mirabilis*), I did not, I can now disclose, wholly abandon the game I loved. I can now safely fill the lacuna between my epic innings on Big Ground (where I learned gardening – but, unfortunately, no other relevant skill – from P.B.H. May) and my cultivated little displays for East Bergholt. I can scotch rumours that I coached in South Africa; nor did I play club stuff, under a pseudonym, in Lancashire. My cricket in the Lost Decade of the Fifties was played at venues which rarely figure in routine touring geography. How many of your standard giants have played at Pampelonne (as distinct from Pamplona, notorious for Hemingway's *veronicas*) or Lucca or Menton or Biarritz?

For reasons which should perhaps remain a secret between myself and my guru, I played my greatest innings, and took my finest catches, on grounds where, according to banal accounts, the Game Never Caught On. The Latin races, so the cant insists, lack the temperament for cricket. 'Fair play' may figure in their vocabulary; it is rarer in their practice. They do not truly understand the team spirit, hence their Many Misfortunes. The French, to their chagrin, always know when they are beaten; the Italians would almost certainly want to wear jewellery on the field. *Non, monsieur: no signore*: our game is not your game. How then did I come to play under those romantic skies, in heat which might have had Denis sending for a cap? No-one brought *us* drinks, I can tell you, when the Midi sun sent mad dogs skulking for shady shelter. Who were my intrepid companions of those dogged days? '*Les noms, les noms!*' the French cry when exasperated by anonymities. I can guess that you share their zest for the particular. I must tell you (and them) that the cricket I played under Latin skies was – prepare yourselves for a shock – a game for two. *Mais non, mais non*: the game we played had nothing in common with French cricket, that desperate attempt to find a use for bat and ball which has neither dignity nor statistics. We played cricket, but – in a tradition sporadically revived in a spirit of Hambledon – with but one player on either side.

If it is difficult to find four bridge players (of a standard to engage the wit), how much more of a problem, abroad, to assemble a quorum for cricket! No wonder that The Summer Game remains inaccessible to the foreign millions who have learnt to kick a ball, and each other, in mimicry of their betters, the Brits! In my Golden Decade I played singles (though I disdained to run them). My opponent – only fools will smirk – was also my love. Is there anything ridiculous in lovers playing cricket? My wife, as she now is, was both a scholar and a beauty. I would, I suspect, have been attracted to her even if she had not been a Middlesex supporter (*she* remembers Thompson at number five and Wally Robins, hurrying to make quick runs at number six, and Jack Young, who once made double figures, even if you cannot), but her modest confession that she had once taken six wickets for sixteen runs when bowling at St Paul's put the seal on a contract which might, in any event, have been signed, if not with quite the same sense of election.

Women's cricket has never had the coverage of other female sporting events. For some unfair, ungallant reason, flannelled fools become travestied tartars when they change their sex. My wife would not, I suspect, have agreed to play cricket with anyone else, once she had jettisoned her panama, but I had persuasive methods. Thanks to her hard work during my Cambridge terms, we took long vacations in remote places, where the horizons and the beds were wide. I wrote (as Mr Maugham prescribed) in the mornings and we went to the beach in the afternoons (the ozone layer was intact and *ambre solaire* basted our joints). We read Rex Warner, Stendhal, Aldous Huxley and *Crime and Punishment*. It was June and July in the south of France. Ramatuelle was an unknown village, whose adjacent beaches were not yet renowned for jellyfish and toplessness. You could lie naked on the sand without scandalising or exciting another living soul. (A lonely Swede used to call out 'Adam and Eve', and we waved tolerantly, sympathetically, unencouragingly at his loneliness.)

One day, I found a piece of driftwood and – crucial flotsam! – the rubber bulb of an old perfume spray. What more did we need? Stumps were improvised and Pampelonne cricket ground was inaugurated. Love and literature can fill only so much of an Arcadian day. Nothing but the distillery of memory remains to recapture the savour of long innings (cooled by the recovery of our strangely elongated ball from the unpolluted Mediterranean outfield) or the triumph of clipping the driftwood with an off-break. She smiled; I frowned, when 'Bad luck' was the cry. How natural was her grin, and how forced mine, if and when the match was won or lost! (What is Kipling to me?) Unflannelled, she was no sort of fool, bowling to an accurate length, batting with a full swing of the driftwood which sent me skipping across sole-searing sand to recover the boundary I had, reluctantly, to signal as I hurdled the red-hot beach.

Years later, I wrote a film called *Two For The Road.* In one scene, I managed to coerce Albert Finney and Audrey Hepburn to re-enact one of our days on Eden beach (far from Eden Rock). Albert bowled and hit Audrey on the leg. 'How was that?' he shouted, without apology, and 'Painful!' was the umpire-batsperson's scripted reply. Lovers in films more regularly play their games between the sheets these days, but there is truth in the improbable, and the ungainly, in the sentimental and the silly and – thanks to Stanley Donen and the two stars – that little celluloid scene on the beach is there for more or less ever, trumping Coleridge's painted ship upon a painted sea with Albert's vigour and Miss Hepburn's radiance. (Audrey was clearly 'not out', and never will be, for me.)

One of the mementos of my youth was a miniature bat with the signatures of the 1948 Australian tourists on it. It had been sold for charity, I think, and was, of course, intended for ornamental and pious purposes only (it was about a foot long, including the handle). The Long Vacation after Ramatuelle, we rented a cottage for two pounds a week, high above Menton. I took the dwarf bat with me, along with my loud typewriter, and we found a new venue on a little terrace, a concrete strip hardly eight yards long and not two yards wide. Under the grape vine whose early-ripening *framboises* (there was a fat hint of raspberry in their juicy explosion) refreshed the parts which no mere 'squash' could have reached, we devised a game of tactful defensive strokes (long before Bailey glamorised them) and restrained aggression which avoided too-frequent plunges into the hillside thickets in order to recover our bald tennis ball. It replaced the perfume spray (gone for an unrecovered six at the end of the previous season). The names of the Australians – who remembers Tallon, the diving keeper? – were effaced by a need for quick runs (three for hitting the kitchen door), but the game was the thing.

At Lucca, a year later, in siesta-time heat which made the whole town available to us, we played in a secret part of the ramparts. Age-old walls returned the ball from the Renaissance boundary with rifle-arm ricochets worthy of Trueman at deep third man. It may be that my opponent was less eager than I to make our funny cricket into part of love's (largely) wordless conversation, but she was as brave as she was beautiful: we batted and bowled as if such childishness could always play a part in our life.

On reflection, although the boundaries were short (and runs easy to accumulate), Lucca was not the nicest of our grounds: the town cats used it for their sport and left it pungent. The best pitch we ever played on was at Biarritz, not long after Peter May (*encore lui!*) had recovered the Ashes (or kept them) as England's captain. The Basque beaches are wide and well-watered; when the tide is out they retain their firmness and dampen the old tennis ball sufficiently to give it a handy weightiness. In the *bon vieux temps*, there were months of the year when touring cricketers could, without vexing anyone, measure out a full twenty-two yards and bowl without inhibitions or cries of '*Merde alors!*' Biarritz was both the acme and the terminus of *mano-a-mano* cricket in the decade before my fully-scored swansongs for East Bergholt. My wife had children to play with, and humour, by the time we went to live in Spain: Fuengirola, then a primitive village, never learnt what 'over' meant before it was swamped by beer-bellied boobies and the charter-flown boobs that went with them.

Did the close of play on the great strip at Biarritz signify the end of cricket *chez* the Raphaels? Not quite. Although the best bowler in the family became maternally unavailable for selection, rumours of her skill excited the young. When we resumed residence in Essex, not far from Constable's 'dear old Bergholt', the tennis court doubled for Biarritz on occasions. The most regular of these has turned out to be Boxing Day (or *après*-Boxing Day) when, with fervent perversity, everyone else's summer game becomes our December ritual. The Nineties can hardly be expected to be a golden age, at least for those of us who knew Pampelonne and the sporting unpredictability of a wrist-spun perfume spray, but – the Great Scorer in the Sky permitting – we shall be, as the French say – though never in cricketing circumstances – *toujours présents*. If selected.

It's Manners That Have Changed

C.H. ROLPH

I KNOW A MAN who has been watching cricket for well over a century, still does it, has never sat in a wheelchair and has never worn glasses. He is called Jeremy, and it is with pride that I believe I can claim him as a blood relation, though here I shall do no more to identify him because he dreads publicity.

He has two other distinctions. One is that in 1899 Prince Ranjitsinhji, having broken all records by scoring 3,000 runs in one season for Sussex, then signed Jeremy's schoolboy autograph album. The other is his scorn concerning the modern belief about the effect of a lowering sky upon the delivery and flight of a cricket ball. This, maintains Jeremy, is bloody nonsense. And nothing will shake him – he was a fast-to-medium bowler himself. He also holds that the LBW law is ruining the game because no-one understands it. He likes to talk about the unique status of cricket as the spectator sport whose devotees live and enjoy it the longest. (Angling, he points out pre-emptively and scornfully, is not a spectator sport.) And he never tires of quoting Bernard Shaw's dismissive reference to 'cricketers to whom age brings golf instead of wisdom'. Unavoidably, of course, he is a cricket bore; but his recollections, until you have heard them at least thirty times, can be both instructive and riveting. In particular, they include the functions of applause and disapproval in the mutual education of a cricket-going public. It's this history of cricket applause, from its birth as a decorous hand-clapping to its modern manifestation as a howling cacophony of shrieks, whistles, bugles and drums, accompanied by the hurling of bottles, beer-cans and fruit, that I am inviting you to consider with me.

The Latin *plaudere*, says the OED, meant 'to clap, especially the hands.' (What else can you clap?) It has always been an expression of approbation and has now come to include whistling, stamping, cheering, dancing about, waving flags and banners that get in everyone else's way, and punching the air with the clenched fist. All these are, or can be intended as, plaudits. There seems to be no similar all-inclusive word for expressions of disapproval, the booing, the beer-cans and the slow hand-clap. Jeremy is specially interesting on the subject of unexplained or esoteric cricket applause, the kind of discriminating but mysterious hand-clapping which is a feature of everyone's first few cricket matches and is usually led by someone with a white moustache.

When I was about eight my father took me to see Surrey play Middlesex at Lord's. This was too young, as my mother had foretold. I joined with imitative enthusiasm in any general clapping about a good catch, a ball stopped on the boundary, a ball not stopped on the boundary, a flying stump. But what did I know of maiden overs and the careful thought and execution that produced them? Of quick wicket keeping skill low down on the leg-side? Of the cleverly-extracted single which would rearrange the field at an important moment? I sat and wondered about far more perceptive and unexplained clapping than this, not daring to join in because I'd seen absolutely nothing to clap about.

Jeremy's education, he tells me, began similarly. Aged nine, he was taken to see W.G. Grace batting. Twenty years later he saw him again, batting for the last time in a first-class game, on 31 August, 1908. The burly doctor was just coming up to his sixtieth birthday; and playing for the Gentlemen of England against Surrey in the first game of the 1908 season, he made 15 and 25 on a pitch white with snow. Applause remained decorous, decent and restrained throughout the life of W.G., who died in 1915, through the First World War, through the Twenties and Thirties: and then, inexplicably, erupted in today's brainless pandemonium. Clapping had then become no longer enough for cricket superlatives. Yet it still seems to be enough at tennis matches, golf, bowls – any of which

THANK GOD SOME PEOPLE STILL KNOW HOW TO APPLAUD.
PARP!

can none the less provoke an occasional full-throated cheer. What's wrong with clapping?

It has a curious history. There's plenty of evidence that the pre-hominoid apes used it as a means of attracting attention or scaring things away, and that it was a method of expressing crowd applause or excitement in times of classical antiquity. The festival-loving Romans clapped a great deal. In ancient Rome there was an established ritual of applause for public performances and 'games', though the sort of clapping familiar to us was less common then. Roman crowds seem to have been good at snapping their fingers and thumbs noisily, though finger-snapping would stand no chance in a modern cricket crowd.

You may have noticed, when the Pope is televised in one of his addresses to the people of Rome, even in the hallowed precincts of St Peter's, that his pauses are often marked (or even sometimes enforced) by a prolonged burst of clapping from the congregation. Christianity, when it established itself in Rome, took over from the theatre the long-established ritual of applauding to order. (American cheer-leaders have a respectable ancestry.) It was a custom of the Roman theatre for the leading actor to call out, at the end of the play, '*Valete et plaudite.*' And the audience did, in unison. This was often organised and paid for, an industry which gradually spread throughout the world and sustained much advertising. (I'm not making this up, there are many records that it happened in English churches too, and continued after the Reformation.)

When Paul of Samosata, Bishop of Antioch, wanted his flock to applaud he waved a cloth from the pulpit, and they went on until he stopped waving.

In due time, or rather a long time, this came to be considered *infra dig*, embarrassing, indeed sacrilegious. After that church congregations would convey their approval of a good bit in the sermon by blowing their noses or humming. I suppose whether you blew your nose or hummed depended on which agency you came from. There's a record of an operatic evening in Milan in 1739, when 'after a successful song there was not merely a communal roar from the audience but a loud banging of the benches with sticks brought for the purpose by the men in the pit, while friends in the gallery threw down thousands of printed leaflets with sonnets in praise of the singer.'

In the *Oxford Companion to Music* the late Sir Percy Scholes tells us how a Dublin performance of Weber's *Oberon* in 1868 was held up when Therese Tietjens, the great German soprano, had sung *Ocean, Thou Mighty Monster*, by a round of applause lasting 15 minutes. It was brought to an end only when she promised she would sing *The Last Rose of Summer*. (Mme Tietjens usually hired an experienced claque which took up positions throughout the auditorium, so that the noise didn't arouse suspicion by coming from one concentrated area.) The orchestra hadn't got the music for *The Last Rose of Summer*, so it was necessary to bring a piano onto the stage. Oberon himself brought it on, helped by five demons from the next scene.

Then she gave the *The Last Rose of Summer*, which is from Flotov's *Marthe* and has nothing whatever to do with *Oberon*. And then, at last, they all got on with *Oberon*.

It is because Jeremy thinks this sort of ethic has now invaded cricket, with millions of pounds changing hands because managed spectatorship has become the milch-cow of supreme sporting skill, that he will no longer discuss cricket except in terms of his two basic beliefs. These are, first, that no-one should ever be paid a penny for playing cricket – this should be ample reward in itself, the conditions having been selflessly supplied by someone else; and second that the laws of cricket, in their attitude to fast bowling, should forbid both the long walk and the short ball. Bouncers would be out.

Jeremy, who had a scientific education (and ought, accordingly, to be a shade more cautious in his withering scepticism about atmospheric pressure and spin bowling), doesn't believe that a ball travels any faster when its bowler has run 25 yards, or indeed has run at all. In the moment before delivery, he says, the bowler's body not merely halts, but bends backward. Even more important, his delivery arm is then swung back the way he has come. The ball is an inanimate object and will only do what the bowler's hand does. All bowling, therefore, could be done from a standing position, and 'all this tap dancing and sprinting' is entirely subjective and time-wasting.

Me, I think there's a lot more in that word 'subjective' than he allows for, but he's too old to be argued with. To him, every deplorable aspect of modern cricket has been a consequence of commercial development, so that he sees, for example, every detail of the batsman's armour, helmet, elbow-guards, gloves, shin-pads, even box, as a badge of infamy and subservience to a hierarchy of grubby accountants. If you ask him whether the armoured knights of chivalry were also commercially sustained, he says of course they were. In today's money a knight in full armour was worth about £30,000. I don't want to give him too much space, because he has been talking about all this for so long that I feel a bit self-conscious about it. But his grumbles now converge in one special lament, so heartfelt and so fundamental that I invite you to listen to him for a moment more.

Far beyond all, he says, in its desolating effect on what we once called sportsmanship, is the destruction of good manners by the current preoccupation with greed and gain, served, encouraged and sustained by the idiotic vulgarities of the tabloid press. Even W.G. Grace, who was not noted for his personal charm, made it plain to all (and certainly to Jeremy, who followed him around) that an umpire holding his sweater or cap was obliging him, not dutifully fulfilling a paid menial occupation. This is a detail of modern top-rank behaviour, one of the cultural changes made apparent to us (and accepted) by television, which disfigures other sports than cricket. When have you seen a tennis star bestow so much as a half-smile or a kindly nod upon a ball-boy or ball-girl at Wimbledon? (All right, Evonne Goolagong has been seen to do it, bless her.) Or a golf celebrity extend the slightest courtesy to his caddy when selecting or returning a club? P.J. Kavanagh reported in the *Spectator* of 5 August, 1989, that 'during the Golf Open one of our native players, Howard Clark, had a female caddy. When he finished putting he flung his club to her, strode past his enormous golf bag, and she picked it up and followed, like a tribeswoman with a pitcher of water on her head, behind her unladen husband.' In which Mr Howard Clark was exactly typical of nearly all leading golfers, conforming to a pattern of truly puzzling boorishness (this is I, not Jeremy).

Is it because of the television cameras that our eminent batsmen, waiting at the crease, chew with their mouths open (until lately they didn't chew at all), and spit round the wicket? This, it should be said, is still mainly Australian; but you wait. I don't know when they began doing this, but I can offer personal testimony that they weren't doing it in Grace's time (though I never saw him bat, and don't recall anyone who saw him chew). The deterioration in cricket manners has been more startling, and could be more significant, than the current increase in indictable crime and arrestable offences. Has all true love of the game been chased out by a true love of the money? It may be love of both, and not love of each other, that makes cricketers embrace ecstatically when a wicket falls. 'I don't think the old players were any less pleased,' E.W.Swanton said in the *Daily Telegraph* of 24 August, 1989, even if, as Harold Larwood observed when questioned on this, 'we just sat down and waited for the next bloke.' There was an early P.G.Wodehouse character who, apprehending that a batsman's socks, visible below his leg-pads, were of some awful dark colour, had to go and lie down until he felt better. If I myself live to be 100, which I am trying to arrange, will cricket still be going on, and shall I recognise it?

Les Taylor

MARTIN JOHNSON

EVER SINCE THE mid-1970s there has been one particular Leicestershire batsman capable of prompting the Grace Road crowd to raise their deckchair notches from the horizontal to the upright position. A wicket falls, a pregnant buzz ripples around the ground, and comatose spectators are roused with a sharp dig in the ribs. 'He's in!'

'Who is? Gower?'

'Don't be daft. I wouldn't have woken you up for Gower.'

And then the roar as the great man trips over one of his size elevens, cartwheels down the pavilion steps and, pausing only to dust himself off and retrieve his helmet from the rose beds, enters the arena with a Bothamesque, gladiator's swing of the Fearnley Magnum.

On the rare occasions when this activity does not result in a pulled muscle, the most celebrated all-rounder ever to come out of the Leicestershire mining community of Earl Shilton squares up to do battle with the world's meanest fast bowlers. The crowd is hushed now, an eerie silence broken only by the master's familiar greeting to the umpire: 'I'll take two short legs, me dook, and tell yon fellow Marshall to pitch it oop if he knows what's good for him. I'm hooking rather well at the moment.'

We are, of course, talking about Leslie Brian Taylor, who on his good days was capable of making Jim Griffiths look like Don Bradman. Yes, there have always been limits to how far a Leicestershire crowd would travel to watch Gower bat, but let them know that Taylor is the next man in, and they'd hop barefoot on broken bottles across any distance you'd care to mention.

Up until 1985 Taylor's batting used to be a very intimate thing, shared only between us Leicestershire folk. It was in that summer that the England call finally came (as a bowler, if you please) and every transistor in the hunting county was tuned into Radio Three for Taylor's maiden Test innings. Listening to Brian Johnston falling about and choking on his chocolate cake, it was as though something very private had been intruded upon. Like discovering you've been burgled.

Given the sort of attendance associated with a dank Monday at Derby, there is a very exclusive club able to answer the question 'Were you really at the County Ground that day in '83?' with a proud 'Yes, my boy, I was there.' Leicestershire 179 for eight and Taylor striding to the wicket – for no good reason that anyone could think of other than that the regular number ten had got himself stuck in the lavatory.

Profiting from the Derbyshire captain's elementary error of placing his fielders in areas at which Taylor was aiming, the maestro made 47. The numbed and disbelieving silence was finally shattered by the noise of the press box phone. It was a friend and long-time Taylor connoisseur. 'Something's gone badly wrong with my Teletext,' he said. 'It says Taylor made 47. What's that? He did?' There was a heavy thud, and the line went dead.

It was Taylor's career-best innings of 60, on the final day of the 1988 season, that sent Geoff Miller scuttling from the field and into the Essex secretary's office to tear up his retirement letter. The distinctive Taylor heave, which normally resulted in a fresh air shot and a double hernia, on this occasion despatched Miller for five sixes. 'I can't go out like that,' he confided to Jonathon Agnew. 'Butchered by Taylor? What a bloody epitaph.' Meantime Taylor, awaiting the return of the ball from some distant pasture, was approached by one of the Essex fielders. 'I know you've never had occasion to before, but have you thought of raising your bat?'

'Why's that, me dook?'

'Because you've just made 50, that's why.'

The Taylor innings I treasure above all, however, was at Southampton in 1981, when Gordon Greenidge had to be helped from the field suffering from an

HE'S RUNNING 5! THIS COULD MEAN A CAESAREAN!
WISDENS CRICKET MEDICINE

uncontrollable fit of hysterics. Leicestershire's number eleven had attempted to run a three, way past his personal-best distance, and a body that was poetry (but not in motion) was having none of it. A quarter of the way up the pitch the bat got caught between the legs, and what followed was like a nuclear explosion. Bat ended up at mid-on, helmet at mid-off, and the rest of him lay in a huge crater right on a length.

It was, I fancy, the thought that Taylor might one day attempt an all-run four that persuaded Leicestershire to undertake a pre-season first-aid course that included mouth-to-mouth resuscitation. The club claimed it was in case someone got hit by a bouncer, although Taylor never placed himself in any such danger. Once when I was watching him through the binoculars at Lord's, batting against Wayne Daniel, there was absolutely no sign of him as the ball exploded into the stumps. One of his more unusual injuries was caused when, he having got himself into what he thought was a safe position next to the square-leg umpire, a flying ball hit him in the eye.

Some of Taylor's injuries have baffled the world's leading medical brains. He sold me a car once, a Fiat, which was an exact replica of himself. The engine was as strong as an ox, but bits kept falling off the body. Once I thought he had developed some footwork, and was relieved to discover that it was merely the bunion playing up again.

Taylor comes from a tough mining background, and I once asked him why he always cupped his cigarette in the palm of his hand. 'Got to round our way, me dook. If you give 'em a glimpse of it, they've grabbed it and run off.'

Taylor won his two caps in 1985 and might have picked up at least a couple more in the Caribbean the following winter when he inherited the Lord Lucan role that inevitably falls to someone on every tour. His best period as a bowler came during his three-year Test ban after the 1981 'rebel' tour to South Africa, but at Leicestershire his bowling has merely been a subject for admiration. His batting, on the other hand, has evoked nothing but love.

Confessions of a Cricketer

MIKE BREARLEY

Editors' note: The following contribution was originally delivered in 1980 as a lecture to the Johnian Society of St John's College, Cambridge, of which Mike Brearley is a distinguished alumnus. It was subsequently published in *The Eagle*, a magazine supported by the members of that college. There it was reproduced in its exact original form. We have made very slight alterations where they were necessary to a written, as opposed to a spoken, presentation. However, we have not altered tenses, etc, in order to 'update' the piece, since we felt that any such attempt would tend to falsify it.

YEARS AGO I used to feel a need to justify my inclination to play cricket professionally: should I devote so much energy to a mere game? Should I give up the attempt to push back the boundaries of academic knowledge? And I resisted this inclination to be unserious for several years. Now, after ten consecutive years in a frivolous profession, I ask similar questions but with a different emphasis. What was it that held me in cricket for so much longer than I stayed in academic life? What are the pleasures of playing a game, and especially cricket, at a high level? And what stands in the way of this enjoyment? The transition is not unlike that from the sceptical approach to a philosophical question to the descriptive: from 'Can we ever know what's in another's mind?' to 'What *is* it to know what's in the mind of another?' We know that we know (sometimes) what's in the mind of another: I know that playing cricket gives me satisfaction. But can we say what it is that we know when we know these things?

My own tendency is to denigrate cricket in comparison with academic strivings – a tendency that had early roots: I remember my mother saying to me when I was eleven 'If you carry on like this you'll end up doing nothing but playing cricket and football' – led me to assume that academics were even more disparaging of sport than I was. Gradually, I came to see that envy was as strong an element of their attitude to me and my cricket as incomprehension or scorn. And one source of this envy was that cricket seemed, in more sense than one, down to earth. 'Down to Earth': the phrase suggests simplicity and honesty, and an absence of cleverness. It suggests physical toil as opposed to mental. And it implies the measurability of success and failure. Despite the advance of all academic disciplines from the mists of speculation into the clear light of verifiability (or at least falsifiability), one spectre that still has the power to haunt the academic mind is that of Mr. Casaubon. Readers of *Middlemarch* will recall that he has spent many years compiling an unimpeachable Key to all Mythologies. Late in life he marries the idealistic Dorothea, who slowly comes to see that he relies on obfuscation, and that her clear and innocent questions make him wrigglingly irritable. Mr. Casaubon's life-work has been a sham. Such a doom is inconceivable for the cricketer. He can't be a failure at his job *and* never know it. Not only is his performance public (like that of the writer who gets his work published), but it's uncomfortably measurable. The exposure is so absolute.

The facts hit one. We cricketers are just as keen as others to deceive ourselves, to shape the facts in our favour. Just as, in the short term, the figures on the board take no account of luck, so the batsman can on each occasion resort to special pleading, from 'the umpire gave me leg stump when I asked for middle' to Brian Close's famous excuse for a low score, 'the chewing gum you gave me was the wrong flavour.' (And however much we who are committed to truth and objectivity may regret it, I doubt if this habit of never blaming himself ever harmed Close, or others. I read in Dudley Doust's book on Ballasteros that the top golfers are almost unanimous in attributing a bad shot to someone or something outside themselves.)

Nevertheless, luck cannot *always* be against one. In the long run figures, though they don't tell the whole story, do tell a significant part of it. Philosophers, by contrast, have no figures to go by, or those they have are liable to be misleading; did not Hume's treatise fall still-born from the press? They can always persuade themselves that a day in the library has been productive. This essay, I am aware, comes into the same category (as the day in the library, not Hume's Treatise).

Naturally enough, the cricketer's comparative freedom from illusion has its price. There are few jobs where an exact tally of your working day appears on everyone's breakfast table the next morning, as a daily occurrence. Winning an election happens, at best, once every three or four years, and being sent down for ten years at most (with remission) once every six or seven. But being out for nought can be heralded five times a week. The indifference of newsprint will already have been supplemented by the heartfelt comments of the onlookers (however few). Crowds are less generous to opponents and to failures than they once were. Their behaviour can be vicious, verbally or even, rarely, physically. In 1978, when Mike Smith and I came off for bad light at Old Trafford an irate member threw a pint mug at us from the balcony of the pavilion; it crashed to pieces just behind us. At the Centenary Test at Lord's, the umpires were manhandled by a gang of members. The Australian golfer Peter Thompson has described how his nerve was tested in an important play-off in an American tournament. His iron shot to

IT'S THE RIGHT FLAVOUR THIS TIME BUT COULD HE HAVE IT CHEWED A LITTLE MORE!

the 17th green caught in the wind, and just dropped into a sand-bunker. 'What hurt,' he said, 'was a sound I had never heard before on a golf course. A huge roar of delight went up as my ball went down in the sand. Hundreds actually stood there clapping. Crowd values have changed. They are not always going to lean over backwards to show generosity to the visitor.' Or, one may add, to the loser. Spectators in a Chicago court applauded recently when the judge announced a death sentence.

In cricket, then, one cannot be completely blind to one's own failure or success, and one's sense of failure is fanned by the fact that it's so public and so verifiable. The explicitly competitive nature of the job can also increase this sense of failure. A batsman's doubts may, more or less legitimately, be played upon by the opposition. The captain of the fielding side gives the senior partner a single off the over to make the nervous newcomer face their star fast bowler. The field is brought in contemptuously close. The message is clear: 'Now we're certain of a wicket.' The bowler applauds ironically when at last the batsman gets off the mark, or, like Dennis Lillee, pretends that a defensive shot stings his hand when he picks the ball up. Fielders show their disgust and scorn at the batsman's gropings. In 1965, as a fledgling in county cricket, I was embarrassed out by the moans and groans of the Surrey close fieldsmen. Such ploys cannot create but can stimulate self-doubt. And the feeling of inadequacy, however unjustified, tends, in any field of activity, to be self-fulfilling as prophecy. Self-doubt spreads. 'What a shot!' becomes 'I'm playing really badly today.' And this leads to 'I'm no good as a batsman.' Once the feeling of incompetence emerges from its burrow, it's hard to kill or drive back underground. It worms its way into consciousness in the middle of the night, and refuses to listen to reason. The irrational voice is soon saying 'If I'm no good as a batsman (painter, philosopher) then I'm no good as a person.'

This argument is crazy, but creepy. It's crazy because of course a technical skill is separate from personal value. It's creepy because if a person allows it to insinuate itself into his mind, its presence there will make him both worse as a performer and weaker as a person. The defect in character does not of course lie in batting badly *per se*. But we do feel that at least some cases of not playing up to one's best, or even up to one's average, are signs of weakness as a person. Let us reverse the situation: do we not regard it as a real mark of character, of courage, to rise to an occasion, to take on a more powerful opponent, and to withstand pressure? To fail repeatedly to do these things is, equally, a mark of some shortcoming in character, and this shortcoming or weakness derives from the burgeoning self-doubt we've been looking at. The deep-seated feeling 'I'm as feeble as my batting' is itself more responsible for a certain sort of feebleness than the feeble batting, partly because it prevents one from doing what one's capable of, and partly because it's a sign of a too-narrow identification by a person with his skills.

At times, and especially when I was struggling to score runs in Test cricket, I had to deal with an inner voice which told me that I had no right to be there. I would then become more tense, and play further below par. The morning after a two-hour battle at the crease in the Perth Test in 1978, I woke up with a puzzling ache in my jaw. It took me some time to realise that it had been caused by the fierceness of my gum-chewing during that innings.

The inner saboteur undermines even success. If I scored fifty, I'd point out to myself that one of their best bowlers was missing, or that they were tired, and conditions favoured the batsman. I would undervalue the strokes that I play well, such as drives square with the wicket, and overvalue those that I rarely play. I would remember the streaky shots.

What is the origin of this damaging saboteur? No doubt a different answer is required for every individual, but one may guess that it could arise from an over-critical environment. Certainly the symptom is connected with a wider syndrome of judgementalness towards oneself and others, in which character assassination has as its close relative character suicide. The judgemental cricketer feels bound to place himself in regard to his opponents as either underdog or overdog. If the former, he treats the bowler with exaggerated respect, if the latter, with too little. Perfectionism can be an aid to improvement, but it may also cause people to give up, or panic and perform worse, because they don't come up to some self-imposed standard of excellence. Hypochondria is another way of dealing with the anxiety of a testing situation, as are its psychosomatic relatives like sleeplessness and nail-biting.

So far the source of failure has loomed large in this account. There are also the successes, when crowds and newspapers flatter. There is the valued praise of fellow-professionals. But we do notice adverse criticism more readily than favourable. And health is harder to describe than illness. We rarely reflect on health or success until the wheel turns the wrong way. Certainly the state of mind of a batsman 'on the go' and resilient is quite different from that of one suffering from the self-doubt that I've been describing. John Edrich, for example, once scored 310 in a Test match against New Zealand at Leeds. For most of his innings, played on a pitch that helped seam bowling, he played at and missed at least one ball an over. But he shrugged off these little moral defeats, and received the next ball with an uncluttered mind.

At times, especially between 1974 and 1977, and again this last summer (1980), I have had a similar attitude at the crease. I have relished the contest. When in difficulties I have, like a toddler learning to walk, picked myself up and carried on without self-criticism, and scored runs when below my best. I enjoyed the bowler's skill. When Robin Jackman bowled a ball that pitched on middle stump and veered away over the top of off-stump, I appreciated the delivery for what it was, and still looked forward to the next ball. In such a mood one can almost (but not quite) hope that the bowler stays at this peak, so that the pleasure of the competition remains intense; one can certainly be grateful to him for it afterwards. After one classic fight for the world middle-weight title in 1948 Rocky Graziano and Tony Zale fell into each other's arms. Similarly batsmen and bowlers need each other's skills so that the action, the drama, can come alive.

The first time I batted against the Indian off-spinner, Earpaly Prasanna, was in a relatively unimportant match at Ahmedabad. He bowled only a few overs at me, and I scored a few runs. But there was what struck me as a peculiarly Indian flavour to our interaction. I noticed that after I played each ball Prasanna would look at me and catch my eye. Sometimes he wagged his head a little. Always he looked shrewd and knowing. I enjoyed this, and started to join in his game. He had an engaging appearance, short and plump with big round baby's eyes. The messages were, I think, instructive about the source of much of cricket's pleasure. The exchange, if verbalised, might have gone as follows:

Prasanna: 'Did you notice how I drew you forward there, and made you reach for the ball? A bit slower, you see, but the same action.'
Me: 'Yes, indeed, I noticed it. Beautiful bowling. But though I had to watch you, I didn't let you fool me, I waited for the ball to come, and quietly dropped it down.'

Prasanna (after another ball): 'Ah, you thought of driving that one, did you not? But no doubt you also saw how foolish it would be to take such a liberty with me.'
Me: 'Yes, I probably could have gone through with my shot, but couldn't quite trust myself on this pitch. Wait until I get you on a true wicket!'

The mutual appreciation in this sporting dialogue is crucial. Each of us liked having an opponent it would be worthwhile getting the better of. We both enjoyed the other's knowing that we were playing well. Such knowledge need not only be between the contestants. The crowd, and those other onlookers, the fielders, can to an extent share it. I once saw Ravi Shankar play the sitar in Delhi. Around him on the floor sat his closest acolytes and apprentices. Again there was the expressive shake of the head from the performer and the initiates' encouraging response: 'A player like you needs an audience like us who appreciate you as we do.'

The character of the sporting interaction varies, and few fast bowlers indulge in the head-wagging and subtle eye-contacts of an Indian spinner. But the essential features remain. Moreover as a batsman I often find that the slight physical risk presented by a fast bowler increases, if anything, the liveliness of my concentration. Again, the bond is enhanced by mutual respect. The logical fact that batsmen and bowlers are necessary for there to be a game at all is paralleled by the psychological fact that batsmen and bowlers have an absorbed interest in each other's activities. This unity of the protagonists is, paradoxically, derived from their confrontation. One fundamental pleasure of competitive games is getting the better of someone else, whether individually or as a team. Games such as cricket evolved to satisfy competitive urges, and are constituted by rules which set out what counts as winning and losing. Sport offers an arena in which aggressive desires may be channelled, with restraints that prevent the aggression from getting out of hand. There are restraints written into the rules – or Laws as they're called in cricket – (you can't, as a bowler, throw the ball at the batsman) and restraints that are matters of convention (you don't bowl even what would otherwise be a legitimate number of bouncers at tail-end, or incompetent, batsmen).

Bits of cricket are obviously aggressive, but much of it is apparently gentle. In what ways *is* this drowsy game aggressive? Clearly not as boxing is; the *point* of the activity is not doing what physically hurts an opponent. And there is no body-contact as in rugby. Cricket does not so clearly symbolise violent loss as does fencing, when a hit would, without armour, often spell death. But loss is central to it. A batsman has only one 'life'. He is given a 'life' if a fielder drops him. And the idea that he is with his bat defending his property against attack is embodied in the colloquialism for bowled, namely 'castled'. Cricket is also aggressive in the way in which all sports are: when you take part, you enter a competitive fray in which the aim is psychological mastery. Such domination can be achieved by subtlety or cunning, by grit and determination, as well as by violence. Croquet offers the opportunity for particularly malicious aggression in that you take time out from your own progress towards the goal to knock your opponent's ball back to the beginning – a feature that game shares with some academic arguments.

Aggression may appear on the field as bristling bellicosity such as we associate with Australians like Rod Marsh. His cricket is, however, utterly straightforward. It involves no denial of cricketing traditions. The English are capable of more perfidious means of achieving our ends. It was an Oxford man who was ruthless enough to adopt the unprecedented tactic of bodyline bowling in the 1932-33 tour of Australia. Douglas Jardine had his bowlers bowl short at the batsman's body with seven or eight of the nine fielders on the leg-side. Moreover Jardine maintained this dangerous form of attack despite tremendous criticism. Most people, and I am among them, think Jardine went too far. Afterwards the legislators outlawed intimidatory bowling (though there has always been argument about what constitutes intimidation). In the 1950s bodyline was made even more unlikely with the introduction of a law forbidding more than two fielders behind square on the leg-side.

The bouncer is the most blatantly aggressive part of cricket. It has recently had something of a revival. Its aim has become more deadly, at the throat or chest rather than above the head like a shot across the bows. The spirit in which it's bowled varies of course. Brian Statham's rare bouncers were bowled almost mildly. Butch White was genially hostile, whereas I've always felt a certain viciousness of intent when on the receiving end of Colin Croft's bouncers.

As we have seen, aggression is not confined to fast bowling. It shows itself in a ruthless dedication to success, and in a willingness to leap over the usual limits of convention. It can spill over into bad sportsmanship; it can be misdirected. It can be hot or cold, furious like Othello's or calculating like Iago's. But at least as common as these excesses is an often unacknowledged uneasiness about aggression. We may be overwhelmed by the aggression of the opposition and/or the crowd, and lose touch with our own combative powers. I have seen England players do this at Perth, surrendering to the legend of Lillee and the Perth pitch. There's a fear too, that showing one's own aggression will invite even fiercer retaliation (though Greig used to rile Lillee intentionally, believing that he bowled worse, though faster, when irate).

Fear of allowing one's aggression full play produces a damaging timidity. I have found that wearing a helmet for batting frees essential aggression in me. The helmet also elicited some inessential aggression from the pundits and from the general public. But despite the taunts, many of them directed at me when I first appeared in the little skull-cap in 1977, I'm convinced that they improve the game for batsmen, bowlers and spectators alike. Critics have argued (1) that helmets would make batsmen reckless, rather as opponents of seat-belts claimed that car-drivers would be less cautious. Viv Richards declines to wear a helmet for this reason; he wants to keep alive that element of risk without which he might be tempted to rashness. I maintain that for most batsmen it's a good thing to be less cautious, but that the helmet does not make us reckless. The critics claimed (2) that the helmet would provoke the fast bowler into more hostility by announcing the batsman's awareness of risk. I have not found this to be the case. Indeed, many fast bowlers prefer batsmen to be protected because they don't really want to cause injury. Bob Willis walks away after hurting a batsman, not because he doesn't care but because he doesn't want his aggressiveness to be dimmed by pity. The helmet makes a bouncer more what it should be, a means of getting a man out (whether mis-hooking, or fending it off, or playing differently against the next delivery), rather than a way of knocking him out. And (3) critics have said that the helmet is a sign of cowardice. Denis Compton wrote that if helmets had been in vogue at the time when he went back in to bat against Lindwall and Miller with five stitches in his eyebrow, he could not have worn one; it would have been, he says, 'an insult to my manhood'.

The most obvious response is, what's so special about helmets? Is it unmanly to wear pads, or gloves? And what about the box? A fearless manhood might be more sensitive about protection nearer to home. Or is it, perhaps, a matter of visibility? Would a multi-coloured codpiece be unmanly, and an invisible helmet not? These days the word 'manly' jars. Women cricketers need courage as do men. So the question should be reformulated: is wearing a helmet cowardly? Is it cowardly to protect oneself against a danger? The answer depends, partly, on the extent of the risk. Some danger there certainly is, as the parents of the two children killed by being hit on the head by cricket balls on a single Saturday in Melbourne would tragically confirm. And wearing helmets has not turned out to be a line of action taken by cowards. No-one would call Botham a cowardly batsman, or Gower or Gooch or Boycott. Nor are Greenidge, Haynes, Marsh or Chappell. All these at times wear a helmet to bat in, and all had previously faced, without flinching, the fastest bowling in the world. When the risk does become minimal – when the bowlers are slow or medium or the pitch docile – the helmet may appear unnecessary or ridiculous. But some batsmen prefer to continue with it so that their balance is not changed; they may even feel uncomfortable without it. And one may, in the quest for quick runs, wish to play shots where there is a risk of a top edge into the face even against medium-paced bowling.

In the company of starving people it is indecent to complain that one's steak is underdone. If the Greeks had played cricket under the walls of Troy, Agamemnon might well have unbuttoned his breastplate and doffed his helmet, however rough the pitch. There is here an analogy with the immediate post-war years. A man who had for months piloted low-flying fighters in raids from which at times only two out of three returned home safely may well feel that it's indecent to guard against the pathetic risks involved in batting. Such a man was Bill Edrich. He, and others like him, may well have felt in 1947 that they were living on borrowed time, that, having cheated death they had no right to be alive. Such an attitude might induce a recklessness, and even indifference, that would court danger rather than rush to avoid it. An American philosopher who had been a Navy pilot in the war flew for pleasure after it, giving displays of aerobatics. He survived one bad crash, but died in another in 1967, after taking off in bad weather. For us pampered post-war (or mainly post-war) children, however, unused to extremes of danger, a sickening blow to the head is not an accident to be relished. Ian Gould's batting career was set back when he was concussed by a bouncer from Croft. Mine has been rejuvenated by the assurance a helmet brings. I feel more confident about hooking quickish bowling. I have renewed taste for batting against fast bowling. The excitement of facing, say, Sylvester Clarke on an uneven pitch at the Oval is still there; but the streak of fear is not.

'Ha!' you say. 'The streak of fear!' Yes: near-misses, and the occasional blow, did produce not so much fear as a lack of eagerness for further bombardment. The adrenalin did not flow so readily in the later engagements, whereas earlier I had felt excited and stimulated. My reaction was the cricketing equivalent of a stiff upper lip: I stood up behind the ball, and took whatever punishment was going. The attitude was 'Whatever happens, don't let fear show.' I did not flinch, though I may have, occasionally, frozen. It's not an attitude to be despised. But I find now that wearing the helmet enables me to be less rigid in response, more varied, more playful, more creative. I can use a range of responses to the short-pitched ball, rather than only one. Richards may need to induce inhibition; an ordinary mortal needs every encouragement to spontaneity.

Apprehensiveness about the aggression of an opponent may, then, stifle one's own, to the detriment of one's play. Another shortcoming may arise from a fear of one's own destructiveness. Some individuals (and teams) let their opponents off the hook when they have them at their mercy. They fail to ram home an advantage. Some find it hard to play all out to win; if they did so, they might be revealed as nasty and unlikeable. We dislike our own barely suppressed tendency to gloat. A tennis player often drops his own service the game after breaking his opponent's, perhaps feeling guilty at having presumed so far; while the opponent, his guilt now assuaged, is stung into uninhibited aggression. The sportsman, like the doctor, should not get emotionally involved with his 'patient'. Neither should he let pity get in his way. Len Hutton's advice to me on the eve of the England team's departure for India in 1976 was 'Don't take pity on the Indian bowlers.' Respecting an opponent includes being prepared to finish him off. Conversely, you really can't escape defeat by the ruse of not having tried, whole-heartedly, to win. Colin Cowdrey, it seemed to me, took this line in a forty-over match between Kent and Guyana in Georgetown. (I was a guest player for Kent). For the first twenty overs we restricted their powerful batsmen well; then Cowdrey put on some joke bowlers, and gave the batsmen easy runs. Guyana played hard, and we lost by over 100 runs. I felt that we lost more face by not having fully tried than we would have done had we tried and lost. Sport encourages the participant both to express his aggression and to control it: to try to win without anger and also without pity; to win without gloating; to win without loss of self-respect. Team games also require the subordination of self to team, and I shall return to this topic later.

The degree to which the pleasure of playing sport derives from personal or group success varies. But no-one could be satisfied simply by success. No-one, even at the extreme of unattractive pragmatism, could deny pleasures which are related to the style or manner of performance. I am inclined to call these pleasures aesthetic, and they range from the sensual to the refined. And as style can't be divorced from function (and the function of, to take an example, batting, is to score runs), these pleasures are not independent of those that derive from competitive success. No-one could be satisfied simply by style, either. It is satisfying to hit the ball just once in the middle of the bat. The batsman feels the ball in the middle, knows with his body that he has timed the stroke, and that everything has, at least at his end, gone well. The huge hit may turn out to be caught on the boundary, but unless the man has become coarsened by the competitive urge he will be open to the pleasure of the splendid hit despite its outcome, and despite the fact that disappointment may outweigh pleasure. The slog must, however, ultimately be disappointing for anyone with aspirations as a batsman. By its nature it's unreliable and crude. Much more satisfying is the stroke played not only with perfect timing but also with economy of movement, safety, control and elegance. By elegance, I don't mean prettiness or style for the sake of style; more the elegance of a neat mathematical solution. And I don't mean that all these features are easily compatible. David Gower's elegance and flow require a little sacrifice in safety. His strokes are more ambitious than most top players', and the critics want his flair plus Boycott's safety. They shower him with praise for an innings full of risky cover-drives (of which he edges or misses perhaps one in five) and blame him for edging fatally at the first attempt on another day. More pedestrian players than Gower also get and give pleasure from the manner of their performance. The exquisite cover-drive gives its executor more pleasure – even if it goes straight to a fielder – than a lucky nick for four. But the same stroke gives still more pleasure if it avoids the fielder and rattles against the boundary.

It has an even more piquant flavour if the bowler gives him few opportunities for playing an attacking shot with any safety, or if the pitch favours the bowler. The aesthetic pleasure is to some extent proportionate to the difficulty.

There is then a significant aspect of the sporting urge which aims at the purity of perfection. To call an innings 'cultured' sounds, at first blush, pretentious, but may be entirely appropriate. A boxer may savour a beautiful punch. He is entitled to enjoy not only the raw triumph of mastery at the thought of his pole-axed opponent, but also the exquisite clean-cut precision of its timing. These words from the language of aesthetics do not feel out of place. In cricket I have been kept going by the belief that, despite periods of setback, I'm improving as a batsman. Clarity can, as in philosophy, replace confusion. After all one's perplexities, one may come to see each delivery for what it is, and respond with judgement and conviction. Getting better means increasing both the competitive and aesthetic satisfactions. A runner's desire to break his own personal record may be rooted in the private pleasure of peak performance and in the implications for competitions to come.

There is always, too, apart from the intrinsic sporting fulfilments of defeating a worthy opponent and of doing a difficult thing well, the satisfaction of impressing others. We do it partly to show off, like a four-year-old who shows his mother how he can jump and climb. Many like public acclaim, wanting to be recognised and treated as celebrities. We walk around with arrows in our sides but, like Saint Sebastian, with a divine light of attention radiating round about (though I for one yearn less and less for the saint's uncomfortable prominence). At a time when 20,000 Australians booed me whenever I walked onto the field, an actress called Kate Fitzpatrick was performing at a theatre-restaurant in Sydney; when she thought of her problems in wooing 200 patrons from their chicken legs, she envied me my noisy notoriety. Sportsmen and -women embody people's dreams and represent their good and bad figures. A ten-year-old boy wrote to me to tell me that if I was out for nought it ruined his day, while if I made a score he was happy all day. Boycott is an example of a lad who had nothing making good in a style without frills or flashiness, assiduous and effective, that millions of Yorkshiremen and others can identify with. We cause a lot of pleasure, and incur anger and gratitude. We have therefore certain responsibilities, which may at times feel burdensome. I feel that my own cricket became too solemn under the load of image attached to the title of Captain of England, and certainly since I no longer have to live up to some idea of what this means I have been able to play with more freedom.

We also play cricket for money. Some maintain, as did Johan Huizinga in his book *Homo Ludens,* that professionalism inevitably takes away the fun of play, that it must lead to grimness and a degree of organisation that together destroy the spontaneity that is essential to play. I disagree with this view. There are aspects of a game that involve, when it is played purposefully, caution, planning and thought. Some aspects are, appropriately, also in evidence in cricket matches played by amateurs on Saturday afternoons. They do not preclude spontaneity, and they in no way conflict with the notion of a game. And professional cricketers play for love. We wrangle – occasionally – over contracts, and grumble, like others, about money; but on the field we feel the same anxieties, pleasures and excitements as we did when, at the age of seven, we 'became'our heroes in the local park. We are still similarly absorbed and it is for that, mainly, that we play. In short, we are still *playing*, without which the most serious endeavour is apt to become sterile. Much of the fun and the satisfaction arises from the fact that cricket is a team game. The rest of this essay deals with the interactions between group and individual. It may also be seen as the start towards an account of the pleasures and difficulties of captaincy.

Cricket is a team game. As such it requires qualities that have been essential to the survival of the human tribe – organisation, cameraderie and the subordination of individual desires to the welfare of the group. But, for a team game, it is unusual in being made up of intensely individual duels. The opening batsman who takes guard against Lillee is very much alone, despite his partner's presence and the more distant support of their nine colleagues in the dressing-room (especially the number three batsman!). Personal interest may conflict with that of the team. You may feel exhausted and yet have to bowl. You may be required to sacrifice your wicket going for quick runs. This tension is inherent in the game to an unusual degree, and gives rise to the occupational vice of cricket: selfishness. But can a cricketer be too *un*selfish? The answer is yes. He can fail to value himself enough, and this can lead to a diffidence which harms the team. He might, for example, underrate the importance to his confidence, and thus to the team's long-term interest, of his occupying the crease for hours, however boringly, in a search for form. And I have seen a whole side in flight from selfishness, with batsmen competing to find more ridiculous ways of getting themselves out, in order to prove that they weren't selfish.

A captain has to coax the happy blend of self-interest and team-interest from his team; and has to exemplify it himself. He must also be aware of, and influence, the balance between individual and group in many other ways. The group changes individuals for better and for worse. One function of a group is to preserve itself against outsiders. Teams have a built-in aid to motivation in the fact that their *raison d'être* is to compete with other teams. A group's natural hostility to outsiders is thus intensified and justified. The group may generate an attitude of hatred or paranoia in its members, in which each person becomes less fair-minded, less self-critical, than he would alone, as group cohesiveness naturally tends to involve an increase in anonymity. The paranoia may have racial overtones, but is equally strong, I've found, against

Australians and Yorkshiremen. Umpires and pressmen can also become targets. A captain will have to tread carefully here. He wants to encourage a legitimate fighting spirit; he may be happy to see an element of group paranoia to further the ends of the campaign. But at some point he ought to feel that truth should be respected, and that total commitment on the field needs no distorting paranoia. My complaint against Ian Chappell as a captain is that he edged cricket matches towards gang warfare.

The group attitude can plunge into pessimism. On one tour of Australia the England players referred to a seat that was reserved for the next batsman as 'the condemned cell'. The team may more usefully close its collective eyes to the odds against them as an antidote to incipient pessimism. Thought of failure may infect a team as it does an individual, and it is part of leadership to counteract it. Marsh tells a story against himself, of a one-innings match between Western Australia and Queensland. Western Australia had been bowled out for 78. Marsh, as captain, gave a team talk to his disconsolate players. 'Let's at least put up a show for our home crowd,' he said. 'At least let's get two or three of them out.' At this point Lillee burst in angrily, 'Put up a show?' he said. 'We're going to win!' He then bowled Richards for nought, took four for 19, and Queensland were all out for 61. When, during the Peloponnesian War, the Spartans were about to make a landing from Sphacteria, the Athenian general addressed his troops as follows: 'Soldiers, all of us are together in this. I don't want any of you in our present awkward position to try to show off his intelligence by making a precise calculation of the dangers which surround us. Instead we must make straight for the enemy and not pause to discuss the matter, confident in our hearts that these dangers too can be surmounted. In a situation like this, nice calculations are beside the point.' Niceties of appraisal and the uniqueness of the individual point of view are achievements wrung with difficulty from the tribal mentality; but in some contexts courage needs to be partially blind, and action headstrong.

The power of the group is evident also in its ability to cast people into roles, with the help, of course, of the person concerned. In cricket teams as in other groups we find Fun-Lover and Kill-Joy, Complainer and Pacifier; there is likely to be a Leader of the Opposition, and a Court Jester. Some find that their only route to a certain sort of acceptance is to play the fool. No doubt a cricket field is not the only locus for their role; a poor self-image may have led them to take this way out since childhood. However, it may become prominent in their cricket, and professional cricketers are often quick to spot such a weakness and to exploit it in their casting. The group may push such a man further into the court jester's part. We had such a player at Middlesex some time ago. Let's call him Brown. At his previous county he had the reputation of being difficult to deal with and temperamental. He was a thorn in his captain's flesh, and a figure of fun to the rest. On one occasion

Brown felt that he and not the captain should have been bowling, so he allowed the ball to pass gently by his boot and hit the boundary board before he lobbed it back. We took him on because of his undoubted talent. Besides, I rather liked him. In our pre-season practice matches he tended to fall over when he bowled, (and this produced stifled laughter) and he presented himself as an appalling fielder, spindly and unco-ordinated (this produced unstifled laughter, though I knew that we would all be irritated if he fielded like this in competitive matches). He also made rather provocative and odd remarks. I decided that we should not encourage him to play the fool, that we should take him seriously from the start, regarding his current standard of fielding as a base-line from which all improvements should be acknowledged. I consulted him about his bowling and about tactics generally. A productive rivalry sprang up between him and another bowler in the side. We reminded him of his strengths when he so easily slid into hopelessness. We laughed at him less, and he felt less need to gain attention in this way. Gradually, he spent more time on his feet than on his knees, and his fielding improved remarkably. For a year or two, all went well – until other difficulties intervened.

This role serves at least two functions: it feeds a (partly malicious) humour in the rest of the team (who can get on with their own jobs seriously) and it allows the 'actor' a (partly precarious) security. A headmaster tells me that in the schools where he has taught he finds the same cast of characters in each common-room. And families most of all saddle their members with limiting parts. Fortunately, however, individuals also resist these pulls, pulls into the conformity and anonymity of unquestioning attitudes, or pulls into the diversity of fixed roles. Cricket itself, too, with its variety, encourages and even insists on individuality. Unlike a rowing eight a cricket team works as a team *only* by dint of differentiation. The skills, like the shapes and sizes of their owners, are diverse (I have always felt it to be one of the charms of the game that it accommodates the vast Milburn and the svelte Holding, the towering Garner and the tiny Viswanath). More narrowly, a team needs among its batsmen the sound as well as the brilliant (Desmond Haynes as well as Richards), and among its bowlers donkeys as well as racehorses (Garner, perhaps, as well as Holding). In the field it needs runners and throwers in the deep, agile and deft movers half-way out, skilful specialists at slip and courageous close-in fielders. Every aspect of the game is transformed by changes in pitch and climate, from a bouncy 'flier' at Perth to a dead strip of baked mud at Karachi. Even on one day in one place the ball may suddenly start to swing when the atmosphere changes. And the new ball offers totally different opportunities for attack from one fifty overs old. So a cricket team needs a range of resources as does each of its players, and playing together does not mean suppressing flair and uniqueness.

The time allowed for a cricket match also allows for

variety and development. Its relatively leisurely pace means that less can be achieved by excitement or by urgent exhortations, though they have a part. There is a need for thought and flexibility. The captain cannot, or should not, work to rule. One county captain had decided before every Sunday League game had started who would bowl each over. Such a method is a shadow of proper captaincy. Mr. Flood, once lion-keeper at the Dublin zoo, was remarkable in that he had bred many lions and never lost one. When asked his secret he replied that 'No two lions are alike'. No doubt he had outlines of policy; but, like a good cricket captain, he responded to each situation afresh.

Cricket's range separates it from a sport such as rowing. Apart from the cox eight men (or women) have much the same job as each other, and that job does not vary over the whole period of the race. Each oarsman submerges himself in the whole; much of his pleasure derives from feeling part of a beautiful machine. The cox takes over each man's decision-making; he becomes the mind for a single body. But even he has few parameters within which to exercise thought. Even baseball, which of all team games comes closest to cricket in the centrality of its personal battles, lacks cricket's flexibility. Its scoring arc (90°) is a quarter that of cricket. The range of pace of the pitchers is much less than that of bowlers. In cricket, the ball not only swerves, it also bounces, a fact which implies a whole new world of different possibilities of trajectory and deviation. The pitcher's assistants, the fielders, are deployed in virtually unchanging positions, unlike the bowler's; for in cricket fielders are scattered in all sorts of formations, over a field that may be circular, oval, rectangular or, very likely, any old shape. At Canterbury, a large tree stands inside the boundary. At Lord's the ground falls eight feet from one side to the other. The variety in pitches I have already mentioned. I will just add in parenthesis that there is some danger that for next season a new playing condition for county cricket will be introduced, whereby pitches will be covered during rain. Such a change would remove a wide range of skills, especially that of batting against a spin-bowler on a drying pitch. For a hundred years and more, rain has played its nourishing part in the vagaries of cricket. We are in danger of trying to systematise the game too far, of knocking down its higgledy-piggledy town centre and replacing it with a streamlined plastic or glass construction.

We have noticed the ways in which a group attitude can take over. It can put players into roles, and cast them into gloom. It can fuel the fighting spirit, or extinguish it. We have also seen how team spirit is a harmony of very different skills and personalities, a harmony that is very often a matter of robust antiphony. Competitiveness within a team may be as helpful as that of the team. Like humour, such rivalry requires mutual respect. The captain must help facilitate all this. I would not have been tempted back into first-class cricket without the lure of the captaincy of Middlesex, nor I think would I have continued to play for long without its stimulation. I used to be easily bored when, between innings. I had only fielding to look forward to. By contrast, the captain is in effect managing director, union leader and pit-face worker all in one. He is, in most counties, responsible for the smooth running of the whole concern. He decides how often and for how long the team practise. He has the main say in selection. He deals with all the day-to-day questions of discipline. He is of course in charge of the tactics. The captain is often the team's only representative on the committee, and is an important link between the two groups. He also has to bat and field, and maybe bowl. It is as if the conductor of an orchestra dealt with the travel arrangements *and* played an instrument at every concert. For the captain it is therefore hard to play God, to read the Riot Act about careless batting when he has thrown his own wicket away the day before. It is all too easy to have an exaggerated sense of one's own importance and responsibility. I tend to feel too let-down and disappointed when things go badly, too elated when they go well. The judgemental self that interferes with my batting does not stop there. I can sometimes feel angry with players when they don't do what I expected or hoped of them, and occasionally the anger is even less justified or useful, when for example it wells up simply because the luck has been running against us. The captain's contribution, unlike the batsman's, and unlike the academic's, is hard to assess. And so, perhaps fortunately, is the essayist's.

Toothle

BILL TIDY

I LIKE WORD games, and if you can guess the significance of TOOTHLE you should be on 'Countdown'. What the word means will be revealed when I've told you about my recent conversation with the international banker and undercover Test selector Sir Johannes Van Hoofenstraater. We were having a beverage at Lord's and after he had incorrectly answered my quiz question, 'Do any of the present England team speak English?' he announced that he was feeling a bit down owing to the fact that a very dear and truly remarkable friend of his had just died.

I affected the best concern possible for someone who meant absolutely damn all to me but, being a keen reader of *The Independent* obituary page, racked my brains to think who it might have been. The obits are without doubt the best part of the paper and *The Independent* is to my knowledge the only publication to have the bottle to actually print controversial denials of some of the more nauseating praise heaped on people who, in many cases, decent folk have never heard of.

My mind scanned back but oddly enough the only ones I could recall were Gromyko, who, incredibly, was given more space than dear old A.V.R. Boot, the Somerset tweaker who never played for England, and Dame Margot Somebody, a musician who died of cellist's rot or whatever it is that these people catch. Old Hoof wasn't into music apart from some Afrikaans gibberish, so it couldn't have been her.

'An extraordinary fellow,' he said, wiping his nose. 'D'you know, he once made love to an Indian Princess inside a stuffed whale in the Delhi Natural History Museum!' I suppose we talked for another hour or so before I poured him into a taxi but what we said in that time left no mark on my memory, for my mind was awhirl with questions. Was the museum open at the time? Did they have to pay to get in? Was it a Blue Whale or a Sperm Whale? Could it be attempted inside a giant Japanese land crab? What other strange sites had attracted the ingenuity of desperate men and women? The subject fascinated me and soon the thought crystallized in my mind that from such chance remarks are best sellers born. 'Unusual Places to Make Love!' 15th Edition. World sales top 14 million!

I decided to write such a book; but hours spent in reference libraries simply made it clear that no previous work on the subject existed and that I would have to start from scratch. From that moment it became my practice on meeting friends or complete strangers to ask The Question: 'What's the most unusual place in which you have made love?' No one was ever offended. All found it vaguely amusing, but whereas men were swift to take me to one side, women showed total reluctance to disclose any details whatsoever! Every publisher I approached with my initial draft was quick to point out that without contributions from women, my book would have no scientific value and why not point it at the 'Last Irish Joke Book' market? The book's chance of success dwindled day by day, and old Hoof apologised for the trouble he'd inadvertently caused and said that perhaps his friend had been unique. I wondered if that was so, for most of the scenes of passion disclosed to me were as mundane as car bonnets and kitchen tables, with just one piano top to raise the awful level of mediocrity. I suppose if reading this has started you combing your memory then the idea wasn't a complete write-off, and it's about now that the anagram which I mentioned earlier reappears.

It was one of Gower's benefit bashes. I'd just been presented with my England bow tie, which was later stolen by a Mexican, when I asked members of our immediate group The Question. By now, of course, it was meant purely as a joke and I only threw it in because all conversation was being mercilessly monopolised by Frank Bruno. They all laughed and offered cars and kitchens. The little knot soon broke up to watch the snooker and I went to the bar. After a while I became aware of a presence beside me. It was an England cricketer, a pleasant giant of a man who introduced himself, bought me a drink and gestured to an empty table. When we were seated he raised his glass and said 'TOOTHLE!'

'Too what?'I asked and he laughed bitterly. 'You know that I'm trying to get back into the England side for Headingley but that bastard Hoofenstraater won't have me!' I made no attempt to defend the Boer because he is exactly what was said but did gently point out to my drinking companion that his recent run of low scores, car crashes, arrests and dropped catches needed no help from Hoofenstraater to keep him out of the team. 'This book you were going to write,' he said, allowing me to buy one, 'do you know what TOOTHLE means? It's the first letters of seven words. The Oval, Old Trafford, Headingley, Lord's and Edgbaston. I've made love in every England Test venue dressing room except one!'

My old mental notebook sprang open at a clean page. 'Not while the game was on?' I asked, my mind racing. Not a science book, a cricket book! They sell like wildfire and that's without a hint of sex. A world market, Australia, New Zealand, Africa, West Indies, everywhere. 'Yes, and sometimes with my pads on, but never with a bat in my hands!' My mouth was dry with excitement. 'Who against?' I asked, 'where?'

'Take your pick,' he replied.

'Lord's?'

'Hmmm, Lord's . . . yes, you might know her . . . her dad's a member . . .'

'No, what country?'

'Australia!'

I leaned forward on the table. 'Now let's get this straight. You've made love in every dressing room in this country except one. Which one?'

He looked at me, 'Can't you guess?'

'Yorkshire,' I snapped without hesitation, and he nodded. 'Miserable sods! I thought Old Trafford was difficult, but at least you've rain to cover the windows. That was against Pakistan. If you're interested I've done all the major cricketing countries except South Africa. Oz, Windies, Kiwis, Pakistan, India and Sri Lanka plus Holland, Zimbabwe and Canada. There's just Headingley. That's why I want to get back into the England team. You know Hoof, can't you put in a good word for me? I'll give you signed affidavits from every Test venue, photographs, witnesses, the lot!'

I couldn't believe it. Cricket means a lot to me yet here was my opportunity to get up there with Jeffrey Archer, Harold Robbins and Jackie Collins, no mean cricketers themselves, and write a big one. My influence over Van Hoofenstraater was considerable and there was no doubt in my mind that if I so wished I could get Sir Cyril Smith into the England team, never mind a reasonably fit, professional cricketer. My cricket conscience was disgusted with me and at this stage I think it is only fair to stress that my drinking companion was not I.T. Botham, and that he just wasn't good enough to fit into the taut disciplined fighting unit carefully moulded by Ted Dexter.

The other half of me argued even more convincingly. It only needed one player of the beloved game to reveal his amazing record and they'd all flock to me. Furthermore the previous weakness in my design, the tardiness of women to discuss the question publicly was now eliminated by the almost certain possibility that the English ladies cricket team, compulsively eager to keep up with their male counterparts, would be more than willing to reveal all!

'You've got to get me back into the side,' he continued, 'I don't want to be captain or open the bowling and batting. I just want to be there at Headingley . . . please!' Several heads turned at the vehemence of his appeal and I laughed to cover the embarrassment. 'I'll see what can be done. You'll hear from me.' He left and I sat there thinking. It only needed a tea date with old Johannes on the terrace of the House of Commons or the Long Room and a word in his ear about forcing Dexter to pick my man. Without going into detail, I have a few things on both of them which, if they became public knowledge, could cause acute embarrassment. Nothing must stand between me and 'Unusual Places to Make Love.'

It all worked so easily. Dexter did as he was told and while my candidate was taking none for 80, spilling four catches and not troubling the scorers, he achieved his glorious maxim. I saw it on television. Not 'it' exactly, but we pre-arranged a signal for those wandering shots of elated or gloomy players' balcony scenes, and there he was, behind the blank, gum-chewing faces, happily waving his fresh affidavit! He was stoned out of his mind when we met for dinner at the Queens Hotel, Leeds, after the game. 'A full set,' he shouted, staggering towards the table where I cringed red-faced. 'I've done what no man, not even W.G. Grace, has done for cricket. More shampoo?' Everyone was looking at him by now, and taking his arm I tried to calm him while frantically signalling for waiters to aid me in getting him to his room. Only one came over, an Italian asking for an autograph, and while I searched for a pen, my companion broke free. 'Stuff your book!' he screamed and, before I could recapture him, dashed out of the dining room scattering diners and utensils everywhere. I never set eyes on him again, but it didn't matter because every affidavit was safely lodged with my publisher and a publication date had been fixed.

Everyone knew it was going to be a smasheroo. Endless TV and radio interviews lined up, advance orders very healthy, several newspapers fighting for serial rights, and when we heard that *bon viveur* and man of the world Trevor Bailey had been asked to review the book for '*Wisden's* Recommended Cricket Books for 1990', we were overjoyed. *Wisden* is like the man from Del Monte. When he say 'Yes!' you know you can't go wrong and my publishers went to great lengths to obtain a leaked preview of Bailey's notice. We were all in the office when the messenger brought it in: the senior partners, my editor and Van Hoofenstraater, who I had that day learnt had a controlling interest in the company. He was the first to open the envelope and read its contents. I watched his face for any clue. After a moment he looked at me and said, 'That blick-haired devil Boyle knows his creekit!' That was praise indeed from someone who'd scored fourteen treble centuries for Windhoek All Blacks, and looking round the room I realised that I was the only non-cricketer present. Charity matches, yes, but both partners had played for Surrey and my editor had seventeen caps and a bag of Test wickets to her name. Hoofenstraater passed the letter to James, the senior, senior partner, who stiffened as he read it, and then passed it to Charles. 'I'm afraid we're in trouble,' he said to his shoes. 'None of these claims by your chap are valid, I'm sorry to say! The whole book stands or falls by him and it looks like he's been stringing us along. Doreen, check what Bailey says. I hope he's wrong but I have this awful feeling . . .'

I waited till she had left the room before blowing my top. 'Who the bloody hell does Trevor Bailey think he bloody is? Who is he to say my chap is a liar? You've got a stack of signed, sworn statements on your desk witnessed by all concerned. The lad, the girls, friendly gatemen, unfriendly gatemen . . .'

I don't know how long I went on but the torrent was still in full spate when Doreen returned holding a computer print-out. She'd obviously been crying. 'Bailey's right on every count,' she said, trying not to look at me. I just couldn't believe what was happening. It was like doing school homework with tremendous care and then when Miss Hastings looks at it she says it's all wrong! My glasses had almost slipped off my nose which meant I was sweating badly. 'Do you mean ... Are you trying to say that NONE OF THIS HAS HAPPENED? He's just making it up? That he's a secret monk sworn to a life of celibacy ...?'

Charles became quite stern. 'There's no call for that kind of talk. No, he's not lying. It all happened exactly as he said it did, and the computer agrees with his dates and statistics.' He took the print-out from Doreen. 'The Oval, v West Indies. Charlotte Medlicott. Started at 15 for no wicket, finished at 38 for two.' My hands flapped weakly in the air. 'Well then, will someone please tell me what the problem is? Please?' Doreen smiled, 'No real cricket-lover is going to buy this book.'

'You're wrong, you silly cow! Cricket-lovers are just as randy as the rest. It's just you bloody stick-in-the-mud traditionalists who won't face facts. Have you ever been in the dressing room with Bill Wiggins or ... ' James came over and put his hand on my arm patronisingly, 'I don't think he understands. Listen, you ...' The others joined him and backed me to the wall. 'The Oval versus West Indies ... Charlotte Medlicott, Old Trafford versus Pakistan ... Mrs Amy Barker, Edgbaston versus India ... Lucinda and Olivia Warton-Smythe, Lord's versus Sri Lanka ...

Toothle

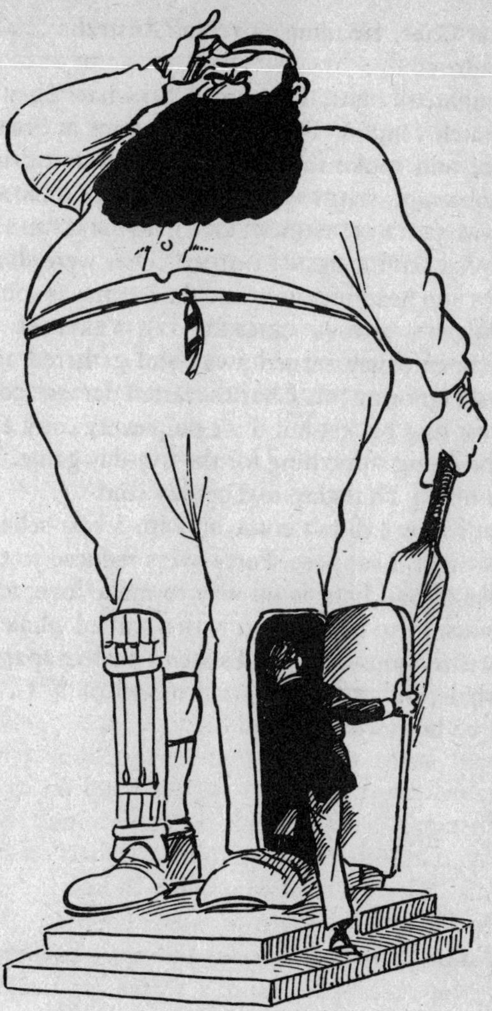

Shu Hai Chee, Headingley versus Australia . . . Edna Ormondroyd . . .'

'All right, all right,' I screamed, 'so what? They're all Test match venues!' They were round me at breathing distance and spoke in one voice, harsh and dripping with contempt. 'THEY WERE ALL ONE DAY GAMES! IT'S NOT REAL CRICKET! THEY WEREN'T TEST MATCHES! LIMITED OVER LOVE DOESN'T COUNT!' They were shouting at me in Sun headlines now and the room was spinning. 'IT'S MICKEY MOUSE CRICKET! IT'S VERTICAL BASEBALL!' Spent, they turned away and gathered around the desk, ignoring me. Charles started damage control. 'It'll cost us a packet but if we pulp every copy at least we'll be doing something for the five-day game. We've got to find a Thursday-to-Tuesday stud . . .'

That's how I didn't come up with a best-seller, and they're right, I suppose. Forty overs reduced to twenty because of bad light is no way to make love, and the trick must be to find a sport with a stuffed whale and a decent-sized museum. Lord's seems perfect apart from the whale, but if a giant-sized model of W.G. Grace could be hollowed out and . . .

Known for the Best

JOHN ARLOTT

IT WAS A wise man who said that the peak of experience was 'To have known the best and to have known it for the best'. The wisdom lies in the fact that recognition is the the key ingredient of the experience. That does not always happen in cricket; when many lovers of the game have seen great players in action they may not have appreciated them for one of two reasons: either that the players were not in form or the spectator lacked the perception to see their quality.

Thus, a boy's ambition was satisfied at first sight of Test cricket – indeed, of first-class cricket – on 14 August 1926 at Kennington Oval, but the degree of knowledge to appreciate it was lacking. Chapman won the toss against Australia, and Hobbs and Sutcliffe came down the pavilion steps to open the England innings. The twelve-year-old cheered, as he cheered many things that day, for not only did Hobbs, Sutcliffe, Woolley, Hendren, Chapman,

Stevens and Rhodes bat for England but Woodfull, Bardsley, Macartney, Ponsford, Andrews and Collins went in for Australia. The Australian bowlers were Gregory, Grimmett, Mailey, Macartney, Richardson; while for England Tate, Larwood, Geary and Stevens turned their arms. This was a considerable parade of unquestionably great cricketers and, years afterwards, the twelve-year-old of that day could curse himself for not appreciating what he had watched. Some of those cricketers he never did see at their best; let us, though, recall those that he saw and valued, hoping that he did, in truth, recognise them for the best.

The first example must be Jack Hobbs – Sir John Berry Hobbs – though his immense shyness came out when the title was used. Once, when I had commented on a superb innings of his, he came out, quite startlingly for so modest a man, with the remark 'Shame you never saw me at my best.' 'What do you mean?' 'Well, you see, you can never have watched me play before the war, and I was never so good after it.' 'But you scored half your centuries after it.' 'Yes, but you know, most of them were off the back foot.'

Reference to pre-1915 press photographs do, too, show that he used often in those days to go far down the wicket to play his stroke. (The fact that he was so rarely stumped is another tribute to his great skill.)

He never seemed to play the wrong stroke even if he did sometimes appear to change it part-way through. His speed of reaction was immense; he was never coached, so far as he could recall, except on a single occasion when he was a child when his father bowled to him and rebuked him for backing away from the line of the ball.

Everything he did seemed so easy and so natural that his skill was not always observed, except by reference to the comment of one of his contemporaries when that remark was made to him – 'Then just look at the trouble his partner's in at the other end.' The strength of that comment was emphasised by C.B. Fry who, sent in first with Hobbs on a bad wicket in the first Test of 1909, could say afterwards 'As a spectator at the other crease I have to say that this was as great an innings as I ever saw played by any batsman in any Test match, or any other match. Jack Hobbs on a difficult wicket took complete charge of the good Australian bowling, carted it to every point of the compass, and never made the shred of a mistake.'

Certainly no man ever made the game look so simple. His 197 centuries – far more than anyone else ever scored in the first-class game – were made despite the fact that he had to spend two years qualifying with Surrey, so that he was not eligible to play in the Championship until the start of 1905 when he was twenty-two, and that he lost four seasons to the Great War and most of another to illness. Asked if he ever regretted the fact that he did not make the other three centuries to carry him to 200, he answered with a grin 'I was glad to get as many as I did, and I never worried about the other three, but, oh dear, my friends did.' That dour Yorkshireman, Wilfred Rhodes, commenting on that achievement, said 'You know, he could have had many more centuries if he had wanted, but he used often, if Surrey were batting on a good pitch, to get out deliberately to give the other batsmen a chance.' It is hard to imagine that unless one knew him. He felt a sense of duty to his county and his country, but he had next to no greed for runs. He met and dealt with every problem that arose for batsmen in his career, notably the googly as bowled by the South Africans of 1907. Add to this the fact that when he wished he could bowl extremely capable outswingers and was a brilliant cover-point, and you have the stock-in-trade of the cricketer who was the greatest batsman of his time – and, probably, of any other – who was simultaneously modest, gentle and kind.

If Sir Jack Hobbs emerged from his start in the first-class game as a highly gifted player, another in that Oval Test, Maurice Tate, was something of a late developer. When he first played for Sussex he, like his father before him, was an all-rounder who bowled slow to slow-medium off-breaks. He was immensely powerfully built, with strong arms, deep chest, strong thighs and legs and large feet, which delighted the cartoonists, particularly Tom Webster. He looked heavy, even clumsy, but when he gathered himself, left arm pointing to the sky, body rocking back and then forward, all suggestion of clumsiness disappeared and he became a most splendid physical unity, indeed a mighty, fast-medium bowler.

One July day in 1922 in the match with Hampshire at

Eastbourne he, like many a bowler before him, became exasperated by the solid defence of Philip Mead. So, from his habitual eight-yard approach, he gathered his full strength and flung down a ball which seemed to leap from the pitch to surprise and bowl that normally phlegmatic left-hander. Tate's captain, Arthur Gilligan, was deeply impressed and suggested that he should develop bowling at that fast-medium pace. He did so. In 1921 he had taken 66 wickets for the county at 26.48. Now, in 1922, he took 118 at 26.95; in 1923, bowling entirely in his new vein, he had altogether 219 at 13.97 and had become the finest fast-medium bowler most people now alive have ever seen.

Although physicists might deny the possibility, many of the batsmen who faced Tate claimed that his bowling actually gained pace off the pitch. For one who did not become a pace bowler until he was twenty-seven, he sustained his remarkable penetration well, and developed late swing both out and in, yet, despite his liveliness, he was so accurate that his wicket keeper could take him over the stumps.

Forcing his way into the England side with some phenomenal performances, in his first Test (1924), Tate and his county captain, Arthur Gilligan, bowled unchanged to put out South Africa for 30. He went on to Australia and in the five Tests he set a new record by taking 38 wickets and, incidentally, at only 23.18. Altogether, in 39 Tests he had 155 wickets at 26.13. Between 1922 and 1925 he took 848 wickets and such was the extent of his labours – for he was an all-rounder and not solely a specialist bowler – that he eight times completed the double and three times – in 1923, 1924 and 1925 – he had 200 wickets as well as a thousand runs.

Although he achieved little material success Maurice Tate was, above all, a happy man. He never shirked his labours: he became the first professional to captain Sussex and followed that, as in a way seemed natural, by becoming the landlord of a country pub and the friend of all its customers.

In the case of a fast-medium bowler such as Maurice Tate, there are a number of seasons in which he can be watched at his best. Truly fast bowlers tend to remain on their peaks for much shorter periods. For instance, Harold Larwood played in that Oval Test match of 1926 but he was to reach the high peak of his bowling in Australia in 1932-33 during what was called the 'Bodyline' series. Frank Tyson, similarly, although he also bowled quite well and quite fast for several seasons, had one *great* series and that, too, was in Australia. Many of the critics were doubtful about the soundness of his selection to go with Hutton's side of 1954-55 to Australia.

They seemed to be proved correct when, in the first Test, urging himself over a phenomenally long run-up, he finished with figures of one for 160 from 29 (eight-ball) overs. During that match, though, partly through tiredness in the Brisbane heat and partly to achieve accuracy, he shortened his run. He had some long conversations with Len Hutton before the second Test.

He had so far been mainly an "arm" bowler which, with his mighty shoulders, had always helped him towards pace, but now that he concentrated his entire physique into the effort, he became quite positively a changed bowler. In the second Test, at Sydney, he took four for 45 in the first innings and six for 85 in the second; and, despite those ominous figures at Brisbane, he finished the series with 28 wickets – more than anyone else – at 20.82. He achieved little mastery of swing and he did not care particularly to pitch short. He loved, in fact, simply to bowl fast, and for several years he had the delight of beating good batsmen by sheer pace.

The classic example of this was his success against Graeme Hole who batted at number five for Australia and who, in the first Test of that 1954-55 season, was run out for 57. His next four innings in those Tests were: bowled Tyson 12, bowled Tyson 0, bowled Tyson 11 and, moved to number six, caught Evans, bowled Stratham 22. He never played for Australia in a Test again. Tyson's outstanding figures of the series were his seven for 27 at Melbourne and over those matches he beat the best batsmen in Australia. For every member of the touring side – a group who always make common cause when overseas – Tyson raised the morale of the entire party after that first Test defeat.

In 1955 a telegram addressed to Frank Tyson was sent to this writer's home. He handed it over: Tyson read it and, without a word, left the house. He returned a few minutes later with champagne; put it on the dining table and said 'That was the news that I have got my degree and we can celebrate the fact that now I don't have to worry – I can bowl as fast as I can, and when I can no longer bowl I can go and teach.'

In fact, and like Larwood before him, Frank Tyson has gone to work in Australia, where he is coach for the Victorian Cricket Association and also teaches in schools. For some years he was an extremely fast bowler; in 1954-55 he was without question the fastest in the world; a sight to be enjoyed– and he enjoyed it, too.

If it is not usual to associate a Test match fast bowler with a degree in the arts, like Frank Tyson, it is equally rare to find a slow left-arm bowler as wedded to serious reading as Hedley Verity, who once spent his spare time on board ship to an Australian cricket tour reading and re-reading *The Seven Pillars of Wisdom*. It has always been the custom of cricket writers to trace Verity's ancestry as a Yorkshire slow left-arm bowler from Peate, Peel and Rhodes. However, in pace, on a pitch where the ball did not turn easily, he was much nearer the modern Derek Underwood of the low economical arc than Rhodes of the high-tossed flighty spin. When Verity himself was questioned on his technical descent from Rhodes he used to say 'We are both left-handed and we both take wickets – just leave it at that.' On the other hand it is fair to say that given a sticky or a crumbling pitch he would spin the ball with any man.

He was a great bowler, his figures show that; but with greater natural fortune they would have been even more impressive. He was twenty-five before he first played for Yorksire in 1930, and after he took seven for nine against Sussex at Hove on 1 September 1939 he played no more first-class cricket. In July 1943 he died of his wounds as a prisoner of war in Italy.

He was certainly a thoughtful man but he had, too, a dry sense of humour. He and Bill Bowes formed a pair of friends from the same generation in the Yorkshire side which, in their joint ten seasons from 1930 to 1939, won the Championship seven times. In his short career Hedley Verity took one hundred wickets in Test cricket in a shorter period than any other English bowler. Twice he took all ten in an innings, on both occasions at Headingley, the second at a cost of ten runs – the lowest number of any such performance in the first-class game – and it included the hat-trick. At Leyton in 1933 he took, seventeen wickets in a day against Essex; he shares that record with Colin Blythe and Tom Goddard. He only had nine full seasons and in each of them took at least 150 wickets; in fact he averaged 185. Every season from 1935 to 1937 he had over 200. Indeed, one can go on through that tragically short career exhuming record after record. Yet he never seemed to be slavishly seeking numbers of wickets: rather he preferred to outwit a batsman on a good pitch and, if he could, share the joke with Bill Bowes.

Tall, slim, but with good shoulders, slightly prematurely grey-haired, Hedley Verity was a distinguished figure on a cricket field. Like many bowlers, he liked to bat but, unlike so many, he was useful in that capacity. On the 1936-37 tour to Australia he was sent in first with Charlie Barnett in the fourth Test; They shared partnerships of 53 and 45 and, if those figures do not sound impressive, they were the two highest openings achieved by England in the rubber: no-one enjoyed the joke more than Hedley Verity. He was a captain in the Green Howards when, in July 1943, he received the wounds leading his men in an attack on German positions in Sicily.

It would, somehow, be unfair to name Hedley Verity among the great without naming, in parallel, Jim Laker, also from Yorkshire and also a finger-spinner. Any captain given those two in his side would fancy himself strong indeed. The first news of Jim Laker, like the last of Hedley Verity, came from the battle zone of the Mediterranean. Sam Pothecary, the Hampshire player, came home from Egypt to tell his friends 'We've got an off-break bowler out there who gives the ball such a tweak you can hear the damned thing buzz as it leaves his fingers.'

Had Jim Laker remained in his native Yorkshire as the batsman-fast bowler he was as a lad, who knows what might have happened to him? In fact, coached by the old Yorkshire opening bat, B.B. Wilson, he was steered towards off-spin. When he came back from the Middle East he still had some service to do, was posted to the War Office and billeted in Catford, where Andrew Kempton, a great Surrey loyalist, introduced him to the Oval. Two matches for Surrey sides persuaded them to offer him terms, though they took the precaution of clearing with Yorkshire that his native county did not want him. How whoever made that decision felt in 1956 when Jim took nineteen Australian wickets – nine for 37 in the first innings and ten for 53 in the second – we do not know, but it must have irked his cricket conscience. Laker's bowling for Surrey in 1947 took him to the top of their averages and on out to West Indies with G.O. Allen's MCC side. There he was one of the few successes, though for much of the tour he was handicapped by strained stomach muscles.

Back in England in 1948 against Bradman's side – one of the strongest ever to make that tour – he created something of a sensation in the first Test by being top scorer in the first innings –63 in 90 minutes – and he took three early wickets. The story is that the Australians, recognising his potential, set out to attack and break him. Whether that is the case or not, his fourteen Australian wickets that season cost him an average of 59.35 and set back his Test career considerably. He and Tony Lock proved a quite deadly spin combination for Surrey, taking them season after season to the Championship. But even Laker's quite phenomenal return of eight for 2 in the Test trial at Bradford, so near his Yorkshire home, did not make his England place secure, and in the next six years he was constantly left out of the England side. Indeed, in that period he only made one overseas tour, to the West Indies, where his wickets were horribly costly.

Then came 1956 when, to all intents and purposes,

THANK GOD HE DIDN'T DO IT
AT HEADINGLEY...
10 FOR 53
9 FOR 37
10 FOR

Jim tore up the bowling record books. First of all, for Surrey as early as May, he took all ten Australian wickets in the first innings; and, with Lock's seven in the second, Surrey became the first county for 44 years to beat an Australian touring side. In the first Test – drawn – Laker had four for 58 and two for 29. At Lord's the Australian fast bowlers, Miller and Archer, gave the touring side a win on a pace bowler's pitch. So on to Leeds, and there Laker (five for 58 and six for 55) and Lock (four for 41 and three for 40) brought England an innings win.

Then it was Old Trafford and the most memorable (or impossible?) match this writer has ever seen. On a turning pitch Laker took nine for 37 in the first innings and, with everyone there holding their breath, ten for 53 in the second: the only occasion on which that feat has been performed in a Test match anywhere. A crucial item in considering that performance is that Tony Lock was trying his heart out at the other end. It is hard to believe that Laker's nineteen wickets – the most ever taken by any bowler in any first-class game – will ever be equalled. After that, Laker's four for 80 and three for 8 at the Oval seemed almost minor events to a public so shaken by what had happened at Old Trafford. However, it left Laker at the top of England's bowling for the series with 46 wickets at 9.6 apiece. It was also the first time any bowler had ever taken all ten twice in a season. Laker himself always considered his all ten for Surrey a better performance – because he received less help from the pitch – than that in the Test match.

1956 was the high peak of his career. He was more than satisfied; and it compensated for many of his disappointments. He had not always been happy at his omission from the England side, and later there was trouble with Surrey over a book he wrote. He left that county and played three seasons with Essex, wrote three books and became a more than useful television commentator. In that capacity he never made the mistake of saying too much, but he always spoke modestly, perceptively and with occasional dry humour. Jim was a quiet man and he needed knowing, but in the commentary box he became the best of companions. His death at 64 came as something of a shock, for he had always seemed strong and well, and he took good bodily care of himself. His memorial is the most remarkable bowling figures, surely never to be equalled, against, most appropriately, the 'Auld enemy' from Australia.

The spin-bowlers of today may well believe that they are deprived of their chance of comparable eminence by the legislation for covering wickets. But cricket and, above all, cricket achievements have always been governed by those who make the laws. These five men, though, were the best in their kind and they were known for the best by those who enjoyed them most. These words offer humble thanks for the pleasure, indeed, the honour, of having watched them at their greatest.

The Case of the Disappearing Audience

MILES KINGTON

BARSETSHIRE WAS A county that other counties always looked forward to playing. This was partly because they usually beat them. It was also because Barsetshire had a nice county ground, overlooked by the cathedral, some tall poplars, distant hills and about five spectators.

'Not much of a crowd today,' said Jack Douglas at first slip to Steward Macrae at second slip. Jack Douglas was the captain, so it was his privilege to place himself in the field close to other people and have a chance of a chat to while away the tedium of the day.

'Why, do you know them personally?' said Macrae, squinting round at the distant stands where the occasional head broke the monotony of the white terraces.

'No, I just thought there'd be more people out on a nice day like this.'

Barsetshire had tried everything to put their gates up. Last season they had even tried to capitalise on the emptiness round the ground with slogans like 'Need To Be By Yourself For A While? – Watch Barsetshire!' . . . 'Get Away From It All' . . . 'It's Remote – It's Tranquil – It's Watching Barsetshire!' A few families had come to picnic, and occasional orientally inclined people came to meditate, but it hadn't really worked.

'Too early in the season,' said Macrae. 'Nobody about yet.'

'Howzat!' yelled Douglas in his ear.

'What's up with you?' said the batsman. 'The bowler's still walking back to his mark.'

'Just practising my appeal,' said Jack affably. 'We're pretty hot on appealing in Barsetshire. Makes up for our other deficiencies.'

It was, in fact, a nice day. Little white clouds scudded overhead like croutons in a clear soup. The breeze tugged at the flag over the pavilion. The cathedral clock sang briefly every quarter of an hour. Inside the cathedral, the dean and the bishop were discussing ways and means of getting a bigger audience in their empty spaces, which just goes to show that cricket and religion have more in common than you realised.

'That bloke hasn't moved for about two hours,' said Jack Douglas, suddenly.

'Give us a chance,' said the batsman. 'I'm still playing myself in.'

'Not you. Bloke up in the stand there. One with the hat over his face.'

There was indeed a bloke with a hat over his face, obviously deeply asleep, who was about fifty yards from the nearest spectator. He sat that way all through lunch, and all through the afternoon session. Jack and Stewart became quite fond of him. 'Our sleeping partner,' they started calling him, and other less polite names. But when stumps were drawn, they were slightly worried by the fact that the other dozen spectators left the ground and he slept on. After they'd changed, they strolled round to wake him up.

But they couldn't.

'He's dead,' said Stewart.

They looked at each other.

'We didn't play that badly, did we?' said Jack.

It turned out he must have been there about three days before anybody noticed. The police doctor was quite sure of that. Inspector Derwent of the Barsetshire police was sorry to hear it. It's much nicer to have a definite time of death, like 11.57 a.m. Some time in the last three days opens up a lot of possibilities.

'An awful lot of people must pass through a cricket ground in three days,' said Derwent to Jack Douglas, who, as captain, seemed as good a person as any to talk to.

'You're not a cricket fan, then?'

'No.'

'Well, you should know that in the early part of

the season at a county ground the attendance is very low. Actually, the same is true in the middle and late part as well. But I doubt if more than a couple of dozen people have been in. How did he die, incidentally?'

'Beaten to death over the head,' said the policeman heavily. 'With a blunt instrument. A cricket bat, perhaps.'

'Don't look at me,' said Jack. 'We value our spectators too highly here at the ground to want to get rid of one. Anyway, I'm sure we would have noticed if somebody up there was beating someone else to death. It would have been the liveliest thing we'd seen in two days.'

'Three days,' said Derwent. 'He'd been dead three days.'

'But the match had only been going on for two days,' said Jack.

'Blimey,' said the Inspector. 'That means he could have been done in before the game even started. But why would he want to come in before the game?'

'Avoid paying,' suggested Jack. 'Make sure of a seat. Have a bit of peace and quiet. Because he got the day wrong. Could be anything.'

It didn't take the police long to trace the spectators who had been at the match, all of whom had been very helpful except one man who had lied to both his wife and his girlfriend about where he was going. None of them had known the deceased. Derwent also for the form of things interviewed all the cricketers who had been playing in the match, though by the very nature of things they each had eleven or twelve alibis.

'Did you notice anything strange at all during the match, Mr Macrae?' asked Derwent when it was second slip's turn.

'Not really,' said Macrae, 'except that once Jack Douglas got fed up with some bloke in the crowd who was heckling, and jumped over the fence and beat him to death.'

'Very funny,' said Derwent. 'Very funny.'

'Seriously, though, have you considered the possibility of this man having been hit on the head by a shot for six?'

'No.'

'Don't. We haven't had one this season. But the last time a spectator was hurt by the ball landing on him,they had the lawyer look into it to see if we were responsible. Upshot was, they took out insurance against it.'

'You mean,' said Derwent slowly, 'you mean this death might be something to do with an insurance claim . . .'

'No,' said Macrae. 'We let the insurance lapse this year as an economy measure, and the batsmen are now under oath not to score sixes.'

Two weeks later the case had been all but forgotten. The police were still 'pursuing their enquiries vigorously' – in other words, they hadn't a clue where to look next. The summer was getting warmer. This year's tourists had arrived and were inflicting savage defeat on minor counties. The dean was trying to persuade the bishop to charge an admission fee to the cathedral. Out on the county ground, Barsetshire were playing host to neighbouring Hambleshire, a superior side in all departments except charm. Barsetshire were fielding. Statistically, the worse side is more likely to be fielding at any one moment.

'Don't see many Sikhs round here,' said Macrae. 'Seems odd to have a turban up there.'

Jack Douglas looked. Sure enough, there was a purple dot on the terraces. Turbans stand out a long way away.

'He was there yesterday,' said Douglas. 'Same place. Same position.'

'Some Indians are very keen on cricket, when it's played properly.'

'So what's he doing here?'

'And why is he so motionless?'

They strolled round to look at him after play, but they knew in their heart of hearts this time before they got there what they were going to find. A dead Sikh. He had apparently been stabbed.

'I know I keep asking you this,' said Inspector Derwent, but did you notice anything unusual during the game?'

'Yes,' said Douglas. 'We got a first-innings lead.'

'Anything else?'

'Not really. We think he had been there for a couple

of days. The other side remembered seeing him as well. Any clues at all?'

'Oh, yes,' said Derwent. 'It's all pretty clear. We're looking for a mass murderer who hates Barsetshire cricket team and has a pretty weird sense of humour.'

'Could be an England selector,' suggested Macrae.

Two murders at one cricket ground is more unusual than one, and this time the buzz took longer to die down, but the more unsolved the mystery became the more it tended to fade away and finally even the local paper got bored. Jack Douglas would probably have forgotten all about it, except that one night he bumped into Inspector Derwent in a pub. He only just recognised him. Derwent was wearing dark glasses and a vaguely Bohemian outfit.

'Travelling incognito, Inspector?'

'Yes,' said the Inspector, looking round carefully. 'I feel happier not being recognised when off-duty.'

'Me too,' said Jack Douglas, who had gone two weeks without a win. 'Did you ever solve the murders? Oh, by the way, thanks for all the plain-clothes police you sent to swell the crowds. For a week, the place looked quite full.'

'Mingle in well, did they?'

'I wouldn't say that. Every time there was an appeal, they dived for cover and drew a gun.'

'Very funny. No, we never did solve it.'

'I've been thinking about the matter,' said Jack, 'and I had an idea.'

'Amateur sleuth time, is it? Come on, let's have it.'

AND THANK THE COUNTY FORCES FOR OUR PERMANENT CONGREGATION!

'Well, I take it for granted that they weren't murdered in the ground, either of them. Too much of a coincidence. That means they were brought to the ground. But you have to have a good reason to put bodies in a cricket ground.'

'Swell the gate?'

'We assumed all along,' said Jack, ignoring him, 'that somebody was trying to blacken Barsetshire County Cricket Club.'

'I assumed that myself.'

'But perhaps that's looking at it from the wrong end. Perhaps somebody was trying to get rid of bodies, and found the cricket club the handiest place.'

'Who would want to get rid of bodies? Apart from killers?'

'The police,' said Jack.

'The *police*? Are you accusing *us* . . . ?'

'Not you. Other police. We're only eight miles from the Hambleshire border. They've got rather more murders in Hambleshire than they would like to have. It just occurred to me that if *I* were the Hambleshire police, and *I* kept finding corpses in my county, it would be *very* tempting to slip them across the border so that they became Barsetshire murders instead. Pop them in the cricket ground. Bound to be discovered sooner or later, but not too soon.'

'It's a completely crazy idea,' said Derwent, 'and I'll have a look into it.'

Shortly after that, Jack Douglas got a note from Derwent. It read: 'YOU WERE ABSOLUTELY RIGHT. IT

WAS THE HAMBLESHIRE POLICE. BUT WE'LL PAY THE BASTARDS BACK, JUST YOU SEE.'

Shortly after that, he read in the local paper that something quite sensational had happened at the county ground of Hambleshire. They had found a corpse sitting in the members' enclosure. Not only was he dead, he wasn't even a member. It was a ten day sensation, with the media forecasting a plague of gruesome cricket club murders sweeping Britain. But when Derwent met Douglas again, he cheerfully took the responsibility himself.

'We thought the first murder victim we found in Barsetshire we'd shift by night to their county ground. They got the point immediately. Now things are back to normal and we look after our own little incidents, and nobody will be dropping murder victims into anyone's cricket ground for a good while yet. And now perhaps you'll tell me how you worked it out.'

'Being a county cricket captain is the only job where having a twisted mind helps,' said Jack. 'I spend most of my waking hours trying to work out the points system and turn it to my advantage. You end up in a situation where a crazy declaration or suicidal bid for runs may be the best solution. From there to solving impossible murders isn't very far.'

'Fair enough,' said Derwent.

And so it was.

Prime Minister Reshuffles . . .

THE HON. MICHAEL MANLEY

ANY ACTIVITY DESIGNED around the concept of performer and spectator draws an audience consisting of five categories. Firstly, there are those who think it is fashionable to be seen at a particular event. Secondly, there are the curious. Thirdly, we have the fans who are present because they know they will enjoy being there. Fourthly, among the fans are to be found those who regard themselves as knowledgeable. These are sometimes self-described as 'aficionados.' Finally, among the 'aficionados' are to be found a few whom *others* regard as knowledgeable. These we call the experts.

Let me hasten to confess that I belong to the fourth category and nurse the secret hope that there may come a time when somebody, somewhere, elevates me to the fifth!

There is a game which those in the fourth and the

fifth orders love to play and which those in the third incorporate in the general scheme of their environment. It is 'picking the best' of all time. The inherent difficulty of the undertaking will sometimes impose a kind of historical constraint in which 'all time' is reduced to some era like pre-this or post-that. For some reason to be found more in the realm of convenience than logic, these eras are often defined in terms of great cataclysms like the First or Second World Wars, as if disaster is more than a punctuation mark in the flow of history.

In the West Indies we have never had enough, say, soccer players of world class to indulge this fantasy. So too with boxers, although the multiplication of divisional categories now puts Jamaicans in the relatively advanced position of asking themselves: 'Is Lloyd Honeyghan or Simon Brown our best ever World Welterweight Champion?'

Recently when I indulged myself by writing a book on West Indies cricket I, like everyone before me and I suspect everyone to follow, could not resist the excitement of trying to pick an all-time West Indies cricket team. Now that we have been undefeated champions of the world of Test cricket for twelve consecutive years, it is an exercise that is hard to resist since it goes beyond a sort of optimistic chauvinism to the realm of choices between players of proven stature internationally. Many of those who are inevitably discussed have claims for consideration in an all-time World side.

When I wrote the book in 1987, my all-time eleven

consisted of Gordon Greenidge and Conrad Hunte, openers, both of Barbados. George Headley of Jamaica was chosen to bat at number three, followed by Frank Worrell of Barbados to bat at number four and, more significantly, to be captain. He was to be followed by Viv Richards of Antigua at number five and the all-rounder and left-hander, Garfield Sobers of Barbados, at number six. Jackie Hendriks of Jamaica was to bat seventh and to be wicket keeper, followed by Malcolm Marshall of Barbados, Michael Holding of Jamaica and Joel Garner of Barbados as the three right-arm fast bowlers, batting in that order. Finally there was the Guyanese off-spinner, Lance Gibbs, to bat at number eleven.

The first thing that one learns upon committing this to print is that there is not another in the game who agrees with every choice. If any exist, they are probably keeping the information to themselves as they listen to the cacophony of complaint and disagreement which attends the discovery that this was the chosen eleven.

It is some measure of the difficulty of the exercise that, if memory serves, I probably changed the eleven some half a dozen times before the printing deadline brought down the guillotine on any further vacillation.

In making the choices I had laid out two ground rules: that each player be picked having regard to the period of his career when he was at his best, and secondly, that this 'best' should cover some reasonable span of time so as to avoid, as I put it in the book, 'choice based on a "flash in the pan"'. There were so many difficult choices between manifestly great players that I tried a device that would permit the best across the years. For the position of reserve opening batsman I added the left-hander Roy Fredericks of Guyana, though even here the omission of Desmond Haynes of Barbados was difficult. For the middle-order batting one then faced one easy and two difficult decisions. Everton Weekes of Barbados was easy to include and Clyde Walcott of Barbados and Rohan Kanhai of Guyana almost impossible to leave out.

The addition of Jeffrey Dujon, the current wicket keeper, was automatic, although some argued that Clyde Walcott, from the period when he used to keep wicket, should have been picked before either Hendriks or Dujon on the strength of his immensely powerful batting.

In the fast bowling department the same kind of difficulty existed. Antigua's Andy Roberts, the wiliest of fast bowlers, and the magnificent Wes Hall of Barbados defined themselves in, but it was difficult to ignore the claims of the pre-war greats like Manny Martindale of Barbados and Learie Constantine of Trinidad. And so we came to the spinners where the choice between Alfred Valentine of Jamaica and Sonny Ramadhin of Trinidad is one which any sensible author would prefer to avoid. In the end I settled for Valentine more because I had to than because I was sure.

In the last analysis one decided this kind of thing by trying to weigh a number of factors, some of which are objective and some, of necessity, subjective. For example, two batsmen like Viv Richards and Everton Weekes are clearly in the master class. Each in his time has demonstrated the capacity to score quickly and with certainty and, if necessary, to dominate the bowlers of the opposing side. Weekes's Test average comes out at over 58 per innings to put him in the top half-dozen or so of all time.

Richard's average is nearly six runs lower. How then can one possibly pick the player with the lower average? Could this be because the deeds of the one are the source of today's excitement while those of the other are part of a fading memory? This can happen if one is too young to have seen the earlier player at his best; but this was not so in my case. I picked Richards in the end because I thought he had mastered greater bowling combinations more consistently than was the case with Weekes. The stocky Barbadian clearly had a greater appetite for runs, and, when set, would consistently score heavily. On the other hand, his record against Australia and England, the major opponents of his time, was not quite as impressive as that of the Antiguan.

Take the case of Walcott. A magnificent driver of the ball, he ended his career in a blaze of glory in that fabulous series against Australia in the West Indies in 1954-55. These were runs made against one of the best and most balanced attacks of all time. At this point, and with Walcott's average above 56, the nod to Weekes is finally decided in the realm of subjectivity and intuition. When I saw them both at their best I thought Weekes the more complete batsman. As to the failure to choose Walcott as the wicket-keeper, I am constrained to say that no batsman can make enough runs to make up for a moderate performance behind the stumps. The wicket keeper who fails to hold the vital catches, complete the marginal run-out or execute the lightning stumping not only costs his side in terms of the runs made by the batsmen who escape. If he does that often enough, he will soon demoralise his bowlers and with them his entire team.

Jackie Hendriks is unquestionably the most complete wicket keeper to come out of the West Indies. Jeffrey Dujon is as spectacular as he is safe to the lightning-fast pace quartets whose catches he has been holding for so many years. Walcott was never tested against the kind of fast bowling which has kept the West Indies at the top of the cricket world all these years. In fact, he only kept wicket for three complete series, those against England in the West Indies in 1947-48, India in India in 1948-49 and England in England in 1950. After the second Test against Australia in 1951-52 he hung up his gloves, being replaced by Simpson Guillen of Trinidad for the rest of that series. It seemed that this was insufficient evidence upon which to base inclusion as a wicket keeper.

These are examples of the agonies of the exercise that provide the thrill and the excitement. By contrast, one is grateful for, but much less excited by, the players who pick themselves. George Headley and Garfield

Sobers are impatient of debate. Gordon Greenidge is, on the evidence of figures, on the general record and by subjective impression, the most complete and successful opening batsman. Frank Worrell was not only a beautiful and elegant batsman of the highest class, but he transformed the very concept of captaincy. Clive Lloyd is an epic figure in cricket history and a superb batsman, but those who watched them both closely would have to concede that Worrell in his prime was the more accomplished batsman, although Lloyd lasted longer and was far better in his later years. Certainly nothing can detract from the record of leadership of the Guyanese, but Worrell was the first one to take a group of talented individualists and mould them into a side that would fight like a team against an adversary of equal skills on paper or, better yet, in the face of adversity. When up against even marginally lesser talent, they could be depended upon to overpower the opposition. Furthermore, the Barbadian was by common consent a superb tactician on the field.

At this point I have to remember that I must not permit the fan to take over from the writer. Were this a conversation with another fan or, worse, an expert, we would be just warming to the subject – if you see what I mean.

Lord's

TOM GRAVENEY

IT PROBABLY SOUNDS almost prehistoric nowadays, when everyone drives everywhere, but when I began my career as a young county cricketer in the late 1940s, we travelled by train. It was the only way Gloucestershire ever travelled – even to matches at Gloucester and Cheltenham.

So by train it was that I made my first-ever journey to Lord's, a ground I had never even seen until then except on Pathé or Movietone News at what we called the pictures and you would call the cinema. As I passed through the Grace Gates into the precincts of the ground, scene of so many famous matches, the place where Compton and Edrich had broken all batting records the previous year, I felt a strong sense of wonder – in that I wondered what I could possibly be doing on this great ground. To judge by the glances some of the gatemen were giving me as I entered they were wondering the same thing, and the net result was that I felt very overawed and inadequate.

By the time I had carried twelve heavy, leather cricket bags up to the visitors' dressing room – a relentless daily chore for the junior professional - and headed for the Long Room to take my first real look at the ground, that feeling had been magnified to gigantic proportions, blotting out practically everything else. The paintings and photographs of famous cricket grounds and eminent players from the great gallery of cricketing heroes of bygone years added a kind of hallowed reverence to this already over-powering feeling. And then came a great shock. I looked out of the window to take my first, reverent gaze at the playing area and . . .

. . . It wasn't even flat! A long, steady slope rolled from Father Time down to the Tavern. It was a real disappointment. Coming on top of this let-down, the generally intimidating atmosphere and, perhaps most of all, the decidedly cool glances I received from the members as I went out to bat, all conspired to make me feel very uncomfortable; in fact, it took me a long time to feel at home at Lord's, to feel as if the great ground and I were friends.

Over the years the feeling of friendship has developed and deepened of course. It began to take shape in 1952, with a stand with Godfrey Evans when he almost scored a century before lunch against the Indians; it put down roots the next year with a big partnership with Len Hutton against the old enemy, Australia.

After this I felt almost accepted, but there were still occasional hiccups to come – a duck against the West Indies in 1957 caused my stock to fall somewhat on the exchange. But I did start to score runs fairly steadily, until, eventually, I genuinely enjoyed playing at Headquarters.

In 1960 I parted company with Gloucestershire and donned the green cap of my new county, Worcestershire, but it really didn't make any difference – by that time I felt almost like part of the furniture when I played at Lord's . . .

With the coming of this easier, more relaxed relationship with the place, I could begin to see the truth: that this was the greatest ground in the world, with the fairest and most unbiased spectators – this was what I had, perhaps understandably in a raw youngster, mistaken for coolness. I was able to appreciate for what it was that special, wonderful atmosphere, which made all players a little nervous.

My most emotional moment not only at Lord's but, indeed, in my entire career, came when I was recalled to the England team on my 39th birthday. I hadn't played for my country for three years, but after defeat in the Test at Old Trafford the selectors decided to ask me back.

Colin Milburn and Geoff Boycott opened the innings on the Friday afternoon and Wes Hall trapped Milburn early on. As I walked down the stairs and into the Long Room everyone began to applaud, and the applause accompanied me all the way out to the centre. I was shattered. I couldn't make out what was happening. If I am honest, I felt that if the ground had opened and swallowed me, I shouldn't have minded much. But underneath I knew too that my friendship with Lord's was now complete. I also knew that Wes Hall was going to let me have a quick short one to start with!

Now that I no longer play I go to Lord's as often as I can, to wander, to browse, to relive successes and disasters from a long career and, especially, to breathe in and absorb the atmosphere that I once found so intimidating. That atmosphere, the special feeling, is still there, and so is the friendliness. And of course, I'm a far better player, now that I've retired!

You Can Take Glory With You

MICHAEL JAYSTON

NO GREAT GENERAL ever arose out of a nation of cowards; no great statesman, or philosopher, out of a nation of fools, and very few artists out of a nation of materialists. The attitude of society is reflected in every walk of life and in every profession. If that attitude is violent and anarchic, we see it mirrored in certain politicians, union leaders and businessmen; and we observe it at its most extreme in sport. For the last twenty years we have witnessed a decline in standards of sportsmanship and behaviour in nearly every game. We have seen it from players and spectators alike – in Rugby Union, raking in the scrum; in football, brawls, fouls on the blind side of the referee, and Maradona's ridiculous statement that it was 'the hand of God,' instead of his own, that beat England in the last World Cup. In cricket, dissent at the umpire's decision and general bad manners seem to be the order of the day.

A fast bowler, recently engaged by one of the counties, said last season, 'Whether I hit them on the head or in the ribs, or get them out bowled or caught – so long as they're back in the pavilion it doesn't matter.' The age of the thug is upon us. His crass comment is no doubt read by schoolboys starting to take an interest in the game, and they are influenced by it. They ape the professionals, and always have done. Last season one boy, playing in a local league match in Sussex, played and missed at a ball bowled to him. It hit his stumps. He claimed that the ball had rebounded from the wicket keeper's pads. Now, it is physically impossible for a batsman to face a ball, play at it, miss, and watch the ball after his stroke – unless he has eyes like a horse, or it is the slowest ball bowled since the game began!

The behaviour of professional cricketers when a wicket is taken seems to the watcher to represent some bizarre ballet, what with hugging, ruffling of hair and the strange ritual of slapping each other's fingers. This exhibition surely debases the coinage of excellence. If they behave in this manner for some run-of-the-mill occurrence, how can they show their appreciation if something brilliant takes place? Some years ago the legendary fast bowler Harold Larwood was asked to comment on these overdone antics. He said, 'We had no time for that sort of caper. If I took a wicket I sat down, chewed a blade of grass and waited for the next batsman to come in. I saved my strength.'

The attitude of the players is not helped, and is sometimes exacerbated, by the behaviour of the crowd and the sensationalism generated by the hacks of certain newspapers. In the old days, with very few exceptions, cricket matches were attended by knowledgeable spectators and there was an air of friendly rivalry. The barrackers on the famous 'Hill' in Sydney were raucous but sometimes devastatingly witty. Today we see many instances, especially in the one-day games, of drunken two-legged Rottweilers baying their mindless chants, whose only concession to devastating wit is to throw toilet rolls onto the pitch. Old-style crowd participation grew from a deep enthusiasm for the game. If you were ignorant of the complexities you kept your mouth shut.

Unless there is a radical change in administration, coaching and the behaviour of spectators, it is not hard to visualise the end of three-day cricket. Raman Subba Row advocates more *four*-day cricket matches. He is a brave man but his opinions fly in the face of experience. The one-day game brings in the money: indeed, that is the only reason for its existence; but as has been pointed out, it breeds ignorance among the spectators as to the true merits of cricket, and has a disastrous effect upon the young aspiring professional.

The contributions of many so-called cricket correspondents betray a lack of understanding of the way cricket is played, or the niceties of the game. A few years ago, to give an example, Botham was hailed by one reporter as 'another Jessop.' Without denigrating

Botham, it is obvious that the writer had not bothered to check his facts. Jessop scored centuries within an hour on fourteen occasions, the fastest 150 ever made (in sixty-three minutes) and had a career average of seventy-nine runs an hour. During most of the time he played, the ball had to be hit out of the ground for it to count as six. Botham doesn't need any comparisons. He has his own place of glory in the record books. But he is not another anybody but uniquely himself.

The press also seem to foster the idea, prevalent in many areas of sport, that winning is the only criterion when judging the excellence of a game. Surely it is a question of how one behaves in defeat that measures the worth of a sportsman. If you can't take a licking then you are playing the game for the wrong reasons. Sections of the press write about sport as if it is a contest between savage dogs, trained to fight to the death. This style of reportage must have some influence on the sportsmen themselves. Darts players point at the board when they have scored one *hundred and* EIGHTY, when it is obvious to the crowd, from watching the electronic scoreboard, and hearing the stentorian voice of the caller that they have, indeed, scored one *hundred and* EIGHTY! Why do they do this? Why do footballers and cricketers spit such a lot? Excessive mucus is generated during exercise, but they only seem to expectorate when they have scored a goal or taken a wicket. Are these actions to emphasize to the crowd how well they have done, rather in the manner of the car driver accelerating after the lights have changed, to prove he is a better driver? How puerile and childish. There was a habit, now thankfully not in evidence, of bowlers pointing a batsman towards the pavilion when he was out. If you don't respect your opponent what merit can there be in beating him – since by your actions you clearly indicate that you consider him unworthy?

The only area where the game is given adult status and dignity is on British television and radio. The commentators, some of them respected ex-players, talk unsensationally, knowledgeably and with humour. There is, however, an increasing tendency to show, again and again, replays of run outs, catches, LBWs etc, which are supposed to give added interest to the viewer. In the case of a controversial decision this can only serve to undermine the authority of the umpire.

The umpire has enough to do already, what with excessive appeals from players, light meters, balls rebounding from pneumatic pads, so that this trial by television can only do him harm. It must also undermine the confidence of the players. According to the laws of cricket the umpire is the sole judge of fair and unfair play and so it should remain. The players themselves must know that, chess apart, there is no game that does not have inherent in its constitution an element of luck. Luck generally is on the side of the accomplished craftsman, but whichever way the dice are thrown, the mature sportsman must accept the outcome without rancour, without recrimination. It is such a shame that a tennis player of awesome ability – John McEnroe – should behave so boorishly and set such a bad example to youngsters taking up the game.

A heavy burden rests on the shoulders of those who officiate in sporting events to ensure that standards of sportsmanship do not deteriorate further. This burden is also shared by managers, captains and committees. In cricket there *has* to be one umpire, one man of courage who will enforce the law concerning short-pitched bowling. If that man does not emerge soon the batsmen will be reduced to wearing suits of armour. Consistent bowling of short-pitched balls requires little brain power, restricts the batsman to a few strokes and is ultimately boring to the spectator.

Lord Northcliffe, owner of *The Times* from 1908 to 1922, wrote a letter to the editor in 1918 in which he said:

> *There is just a touch of English hypocrisy in avoiding any reference to the fact that before the war [1914-18] cricket was dying, largely because of the canker of professionalism and gate money.*

One year later he was writing:

> *I suppose we are right in giving so much space to cricket, though I am told by those who have been to see them, that most of the county matches are poorly attended, and chiefly by old men.*

Seventy-odd years later those remarks could apply today in most respects. In his first letter he could be writing of one-day cricket, which seems to be the child of its age. Compared to the county game and the Test matches, one-day cricket requires a short attention span, it ruins younger players – batsmen cannot in most instances build a long innings, bowlers bowl for containment. Fielding in these matches is the only area which does not differ from the main game. The player's life-span is shortened, surely, by this surfeit of matches, and we miss the late-maturing glory that characterised the batting of Hobbs, Grace, George Gunn; the all-round skill of Hirst and Rhodes; all of whom played when they were fifty years of age and beyond.

The essence of a great game can only be expressed by the people who play it. It is my belief that a person's character is revealed to the full by the way he conducts himself in sporting activity.

The deeper and richer a game is, the more opportunity there is to infuse it with one's own personality, by way of style, wit and imagination.

With the exception of chess, cricket is the most complex game ever devised. George Bernard Shaw wrote, 'The English had no concept of eternity, so they invented cricket.' The other day I was reminded of the rich beauty and power of cricket while listening to an old tape recording of Sir Robert Menzies, then Prime Minister of Australia. Sir Robert attended the Lord's Test, England versus Australia, 1968, in the company of Wilfred Rhodes, who in the estimation of many experts would rank as the greatest all-round cricketer of all time. Rhodes was seventy-two years of age, and blind, but Menzies said that Rhodes could describe many of the shots that were played and the balls that were bowled – he could see them in his mind's eye. It must be a beautiful game if it can accompany a man into blindness and provide him with memories in his imagination for the rest of his life.

Rhodes, after the Leeds Test of 1956, was travelling home with his daughter on a train full of people talking about the game. One of them looked at the quiet figure in the corner and whispered to the lady with him:

'Is he your dad?'

'Yes.'

'Blind, isn't he?'

'Yes.'

'Does he know anything about cricket?'

'A bit.'

'Good. You ought to take him to a match or two and explain things to him. It would do him the world of good to have an interest.'

'And there I was in my corner,' said Rhodes, 'and I never said a word.'

From the sanity and dignity of a great player to the insanity of Hitler. It must be a powerful game if Hitler had to ban it in 1934. His reasons were that it was decadent and effeminate. Oh, to turn back the clock and have the psychopathic little clown in the nets facing Botham and Lillee and Trueman and Tyson.

There is a dearth of eccentrics or humorists in society in general and in cricket in particular. It is vital that we try and preserve this dying breed. Today cricket is becoming debased by its lack of characters and confined in the area of humour. It is said in many quarters that there is more pressure on cricketers nowadays than there used to be in the past. It is hard to imagine more pressure than that endured by the salt-of-the-earth county pros of years past – poor wages, no coaching engagements in the winter, the onus on them to average thirty or more every season, or take forty-odd wickets, year in year out, with never the hope of playing for England. That is pressure. Yet humour and eccentricity were alive, shared by amateur and professional alike. They weren't, however, anarchic. Discipline still prevailed.

It prevailed in that far-flung corner of the cricketing world, Hollywood, when Sir C. Aubrey Smith, the ex-Sussex and England captain, in charge of an expatriate eleven, sent Errol Flynn off the field for not having all his shirt buttons fastened. 'You are not playing a pirate, you are playing cricket,' he bellowed. Flynn went off the field, meek as a lamb, and returned a few minutes later suitably dressed. For all his rebelliousness in other areas he realised that cricket had a protocol. He also had his career to think of. The American producers knew that in an Englishman cricket inspired the same reverence as the World Series.

Sir Aubrey was still captaining the Hollywood Cricket Club when he was over seventy years of age. There was an occasion during this time when he dropped a simple catch at slip. Sir Aubrey stopped the game and shouted for his butler. 'Fetch my glasses,' was his order. The game was halted until the butler appeared from the pavilion with the said glasses on a silver tray. Sir Aubrey put them on and play was allowed to continue. Next ball, Sir Aubrey missed another easy slip chance. There was a deathly hush until Sir Aubrey bellowed at the retreating butler, 'You damn fool, you brought me my reading glasses!'

It is a far cry from the plushness of Hollywood, butlers and champagne to a mining village in Nottingham; but that is the link between an aristocratic eccentric and a salt-of-the-earth Notts batsman – by name, Charlie Harris, who ranks top of the list in most cricket writers' estimates when it comes to humorous characters. Charlie was no mean bat either, sharing in 46 opening century stands with Walter Keeton, but it is as one of the last genuine characters of the game that he will be remembered. His favourite pastime was dressing up as a policeman, complete with false moustache, and accusing newly arrived young ground staff members of implication in some robbery or gruesome murder. Kippers would be found in team-mates' cricket bags. Letters would arrive from the MCC (forged by Charlie) inviting numerous colleagues on tours of Iceland and Borneo.

There was the occasion against Essex, when Charlie and his opening partner Walter Keeton had to open the innings for the last half hour of the day's play. Visibility was poor (this was in the days before light meters) and Charlie had voiced some quiet words of protest with the umpires – to no avail. Out they went to bat, Keeton walking towards the wicket, Charlie meandering at an angle towards the nets with a torch in one hand. After being eventually guided to the stumps, Charlie squinted down the pitch and said, 'Is that you, Frank?' – the umpire was in fact Joe Hills – and then, 'I'll turn my bat sideways so the pavilion lights don't blind you off the reflection.' In the end he said 'Frank, could you ask them to turn the lights off? They're very distracting.'

'All right, Charlie, you win,' said the umpire, and off they came. Nowadays the press would get the wrong end of the story and Charlie would probably be hauled up in front of some committee charged with bringing the game into disrepute, fined and warned about future behaviour. It is sad that no room can be found for the genial maverick, who by his basic humanity can only enrich the game.

From Charlie Harris to another legendary humorist and great batsman. The name of George Gunn must always be mentioned in a list of cricket eccentrics. My favourite story concerns a match at Worcester against Notts in 1929. George and his partner 'Dodge' Whysall were respectively 16 and 17 not out overnight. George said, in a recording years later:

'We went to the music hall, got back to the hotel, had dinner and a few drinks. At a few minutes past twelve Whysall looked at the clock and said "George, it's your birthday today," and he brought out some music – "Watchman, what of the night?", Iolanthe and some dance tunes. Well, we stayed up singing songs and the sun was shining like billy-o when we went to bed. Next day when we went out to bat I said "Are you all right?," and Whysall said "Yes, I'm all right," although he only had one eye open. He got about seventy, and I carried on, and happened to get a hundred on my birthday.'

'Happened to get a hundred on my birthday.' What understatement! It was his *fiftieth* birthday. Perhaps they had stronger stomachs for drink in those days, or maybe Gilbert and Sullivan is an antidote to a bibulous night. Or could it be that George Gunn had a technique and vast experience that was not affected by an occasional late night? How would George have batted to the strains of 'Ere we go'? He would probably have worn earplugs.

Why does one have to search back down the years to find humorous eccentrics? There do not seem to be any in the game today. Admittedly cricketers of past times were not spied on by the gutter press. Sportsmen did not have to deny allegations that they had had a few drinks or been with a go-go dancer the night before a game. Is it the media who try to reduce them with their hounding and lies and half-truths? The way David Gower was treated by sections of the press in 1989 was shameful, especially when one considers that he is the only English batsman with style that we have.

Botham was once quoted as saying 'Too many people in cricket live in the past.' The past is always with us, hopefully signposting the way to the future. There are more books written about cricket than any other sport. This literature exists because the lovers of the game want to savour once more contests they may have seen, astonishing batting or bowling feats. Games that they have not witnessed can come alive when penned by the knowledgeable writer.

Surely Botham would want us to remember his past achievements? 1981 will remain forever etched in the minds of all cricket followers as the year in which Botham, against all the odds, took on the Australians in the third Test match at Leeds when the game seemed utterly lost. A whole book has been written about this Test series, but briefly the facts are that Botham came to the wicket with England needing 92 to avoid an innings defeat, with three wickets left. Botham scored 149 not out. The Australians were demoralised and Willis polished them off in the second innings. 'Against all odds.' The odds to be exact were 500-1 against England winning, as quoted by Ladbrokes. Ladbrokes have never again dared to quote a figure anywhere near this on a cricket result, owing to Botham's amazing exploits. In the fourth Test at Birmingham England won again when all seemed lost, mainly because Botham took five wickets in the second innings for 11 runs! These two matches alone would have been enough for any ordinary mortal to retire on. The Manchester Test following saw Botham score 118 runs in 123 minutes, coming to the wicket when England were 104-5. Included in this score was a savage attack on Lillee and Alderman, who on taking the new ball conceded 66 runs off eight overs. Botham also took four catches and five wickets. If this had been a fictional story written by a schoolboy the reader would have thought it ridiculous, beyond the realms of possibility.

Wisden put it succinctly: 'Botham stretched the bounds of logic and belief.' 1981 now belongs firmly in that past of which Botham talked. Does he want the cricketing public to forget that memorable year? He is on a losing wicket. Every time his name is mentioned, the greybeards will tell the youngsters, and if Fate is kind and he reaches a noble old age, he will have to recount again and again to his grandchildren how, 'against all the odds,' he carved his name in cricket history.

The essence of Botham's performances that year could be summed up in some lines from the film *They Died With Their Boots On*. Errol Flynn, he of the unbuttoned shirt, played General Custer. In one scene he has a drinking contest with someone whom he knows to be a traitor. The traitor says that Custer will be outnumbered in the battle to come. Custer says:

'The greater the odds, the greater the glory. Come on, let's drink to glory.'

To which the traitor replies:

'What did glory ever get you but a two-bit job and a court martial? Well that's not enough. Now we're going to drink to something that's worth having. Something they'll kiss your feet for having. Here's to money and long may she jingle.'

They drink, and then Custer says:

...STAND WAS BROKEN IMMEDIATELY AFTER TEA
WHEN A FAST INSWINGER FROM S. BULL
AT THE LITTLE BIG HORN END...

'You may be right about money, quite right. But there's one thing to be said for glory.'

'What's that?'

'You can take glory with you – when it's your time to go.'

Obviously professional cricketers need to earn money, but what value could one have put on the contribution of Botham in 1981? Ten sacks of potatoes? Twenty-six camels? Four Mercedes? Or was it priceless? We cannot be fixed in our ideas like flies in aspic, with times and players of the past, but many aspects of the game are constant and will remain so. The aspirations of batting and bowling excellence have not changed one iota in terms of technique in 150 years. It is strange that many players already of Test status have to be coached nowadays to bowl and bat properly, when they should have learnt the basics in their teens.

If cricket as we know it is to pass from life into history we hope it will not be by the slow process of dispersion and decay. Radical methods of correction are needed to halt the process. Individuality must be encouraged, not stifled. We see in English football and tennis stereotyped ideas, bereft of imagination.

In the cricket sphere Botham has been the only home-grown genuine all-rounder to emerge for a long time. Not everyone can play with that degree of flamboyance, panache and skill, but if the seeds are sown in the right environment we could see a revival of English cricket.

We need decent wickets above all. On bad wickets

an ordinary medium-pace bowler seems a world-beater. We need committees packed with ex-professionals, not staffed, as many of them are, with people who have bought their way to that position. We need captains who temper discipline with fairness. In 1960-61 (to visit the past once more) Frank Worrell and Richie Benaud captained their sides in one of the most exciting Test series ever seen. The attendance on the second day of the fifth Test was 90,800. Is it beyond the intelligence and capabilities of cricket's governing bodies to capture audiences of that magnitude again?

The essence of a great game, at the highest level, should be indeed not only the exhibition of technical excellence, but the character and personality of the players involved. When style and individuality are not encouraged the game becomes soulless. The sickness facing cricket is obvious for all to see. If it is not cured soon, cricket will become a third-rate game, played by automata, watched by the ignorant. The situation can be saved, but it will need a monumental effort by all those who love the game for this to be achieved. If the spirit of renaissance can be generated, there will be some hope of seeing, once more, sportsmanship, elegance and humour and a great game restored to its rightful place.

Mr and Mrs Fry

RICHARD GORDON

TEN O'CLOCK, ANY lovely summer Saturday morning between the Wars.

Two lines of bluejackets, bell-bottoms pressed, caps pipeclayed, lanyards scrubbed, boots agleam, paraded for kit inspection. The ship's band – famous for miles – pipes up a jolly tune.

'Atten*shun*!' Salutes.

The ship's officers approach, headed by the Captain, Beatrice.

'Show *teeth*!'

One . . . two . . . three! Toothbrush to lower lip, bristling, with the precision of the Guards presenting arms.

'Show boot*laces*!'

Up bell-bottoms to a man. The matelots were twelve-to sixteen-year-olds, crew of the training ship *Mercury*. This was a Victorian house, a drill square and – moored in the Hamble nearby – TS *President*, *née* HMS *Gannet*, a sloop of 1878, dismasted and decked stem to stern in a corrugated iron shed, where the hands lived summer and winter.

Beatrice Fry ran the ship, as tight as a sail-maker's eye-splice. Astern of her, uniformed as a Captain RNR (Hon), ambled sixtyish CB. It is all in a fascinating book by the *Mercury* old boy Ronald Morris, which reflects with enviable humour and tenderness Mr and Mrs Fry, and our world before it was changed in a split second at Hiroshima.

'Show pyja*mas*!'

Pea-jacketed, brass-buttoned, red-stockinged Beatrice sniffs the crutch of each trouser-bottom for evidence of pubescent sex-life. This aroused horror unbelievable in an age which daily enjoys news of sex romps conducted almost everywhere between absolutely everyone. According to Dr Acton, the Victorian Shere Hite, it caused apathy, loss of memory, irritability, incoherence, chronic dementia and drivelling idiocy, acne and damp hands. To spare her charges such vexations, Beatrice had the order thundered: 'Crew to witness punishment!' The lad was marched to the gym, stripped to a pair of purpose-made cotton shorts, paraded down the ranks, lashed to a gun, and given twelve to twenty-four cuts by one Petty Officer, entered into the scorebook by another.

Less specific delinquency was countered by a boxing match with a boy twice the size, no referee, no bell, continuing until loser and ring were punitively spattered with blood.

The boys froze away wintry nights in hammocks slung aboard their corrugated iron Ark. Even midsummer nights' dreams were broken by 'Abandon ship!', the command for lifeboat drill utterable at any time of day or night at the whim of normally sadistic ex-Navy Petty Officers. Everything wooden was scrubbed till it gleamed like marble. Everything brass was polished till it shamed the sun. Their porridge was served and eaten like Oliver Twist's. Nobody dared slump or slouch. They watched cricket in neat rows, sitting bolt upright with folded arms. They were admiringly inspected by King George VI and Winston Churchill. The tuck shop was open on Thursdays.

'The Future Royal Navy', CB captions a photograph of himself amid an admiring juvenile circle. *Mercury* boys were certainly snapped up by both Royal and Merchant Navies, in which they did frightfully well: they arrived on the ships already knowing the ropes. Their ridiculously tough schooling was to 'form character' – an exercise still performed with unchallenged approval, but which I suspect illustrates Bernard Shaw's remark that an Englishman thinks he is moral when he is only uncomfortable.

Though Tom Brown's schooldays were a century past, the public schools were still providing involuntary masochism at great expense. To be fair, the rigorous regimen brought one priceless gift. Two British officers, prisoners of the Japanese, ragged, starved, slave-driven, beaten, reputedly kept alive by consoling each other every morning, 'Well, it's not as bad as Marlborough.'

Beatrice was born fourteen Julys after W.G. Grace, at Guildford. What a gel!

Her father was Master of the Cotswold Hounds. At fifteen, in 1877, she aroused the passion of the rich and randy Charles Hoare. He was senior partner of Hoare's Bank, which still flourishes in London as a gentlemanly concern, with cheques printed in copperplate and staff of unfathomable politeness, where money is regarded as a regrettable necessity.

Teenage Beatrice was already an 'accomplished equestrienne' when she suffered an unlucky fall at Cirencester. She was taking a fence – stone stile and ditch – when her horse stumbled and threw her on the head.

Alarm! Action!

She was hastily carried by litter to the nearest building: the country house of Charles Hoare. The urgently summoned 'medical gentleman' found her not as desperately injured as feared. But he ordered her to bed, in the room above Charles's wife's. Charles crept upstairs every night. Beatrice spent four months undergoing similar misfortunes and treatments, giving a new dimension to the term 'accident prone'.

As prophylaxis against further falls in the hunting field, Beatrice's father forthrightly created her a ward of court. He was so furious at Charles Hoare that he could hardly bring himself to borrow money off him (Dad was always broke). Beatrice and Charles upped and cohabited. Their chaperon was Uncle Fitz, with a hook hand, collected in the Crimea. Beatrice had a baby. Dad felt things were really getting out of control. He had Charles and Beatrice up in court, they faced prison for contempt, but got away with costs. The scandal in society matched that in *Mercury* at ejaculations in the hammocks. Perhaps there was a connection.

In 1888 Charles Hoare founded a boys' training ship, for no particular reason. She was moored off the Isle of Wight and filled with 'street arabs' from Tooting. It was Beatrice's fresh hunting fields. She became a sailor as zealous as Nelson, rowing the boats, swinging the lead, boxing the compass, climbing the rigging and not falling off even once. She cut her hair and wore male drag. After ten years of it, Charles Hoare wandered back to his dying wife and Beatrice married C.B. Fry, whom she had met playing cricket.

J.B. Priestley called C.B. Fry a characteristic Englishman. He was more a characteristic Dornford Yates creation. Yates's heroes combined action with farce and entertainment with fantasy, as speedily and smoothly as a Bugatti gearbox. CB wore a monocle, a self-designer Norfolk jacket and trousers buttoning above the ankle. He was called the handsomest man in England, photographed full frontal (with what Monty Python called the naughty bits glossed over) and was on Wills's cigarette cards.

He was good at everything: long jump, sprinting, rugger, soccer (which he perceptively foresaw as 'A game for the proletariat, appealing only to people with blank minds'). He laced his cricket reports for the *Evening Standard* with classical Greek, while his chauffeur bore champagne to the press box from the ice bucket in the Rolls. His autobiography *Life Worth Living – Some Phases of an Englishman* is as dull a read as an old county scorecard.

He lived round the corner from me.

We have been playing cricket for 250 years on Chislehurst Common, opposite Camden House (now a golf club). Here young CB encountered the exiled Empress Eugenie – 'a slim little lady with a sunshade and beautiful violet eyes' – and the Prince Imperial (now the local pub). CB moved two stops down the South Eastern Railway to Orpington and went up to Oxford with Max Beerbohm, who became the Incomparable Max, and F.E. Smith, who became Lord Chancellor.

CB came top of the scholarship roll at Wadham, ahead of FE, and got a first in Mods. He rather looked down on FE, who had only 'a small allowance from home'. (An Oxford man needed £250 a year, £400 if he felt like cutting a dash.) He assessed FE: 'a fair classical scholar for his age, who scraped a first in law more by native ingenuity than by acquired knowledge'. *That's* what your lawyer wants!

The young barrister was famed for telling a judge: 'The difference between us is that I am trying to be offensive and you can't help it'; for observing to the porter at the Athenaeum, where he regularly had a pee, though not a member: 'Oh, it's a club too, is it?'; and for saving the neck of Crippen's mistress Ethel le Neve without calling a single witness, by a single speech in a single day. The judge later criticised that he didn't even call his client. 'I knew what she would say,' FE told him. 'You do not.'

The *Dictionary of National Biography* decides that CB: 'made his greatest contribution to the lives of others' in inspiring *Mercury*.

Beatrice inspired it. CB interfered little, except for a

perfunctory weekly inspection. He did not even watch the floggings. He mentions Beatrice sparsely in his autobiography, always as 'Madam', as though he were her butler. He gives barely more space in the book to *Mercury* than to Hitler.

The Germans set a clever field for him. They wanted to amalgamate their Hitler Youth with our Boy Scouts (further illustration of the lunacy of Nazi thinking is unnecessary). A 'blonde lady in black' invited CB to Berlin. This ersatz Marlene Dietrich passed him to Hess, a 'very presentable adjutant, he stands well over six feet tall, spare and powerful, with attractive blue eyes, clean-cut features and charm of manner'. CB met von Ribbentrop and top Nazis, several of whom we hanged twelve years later. He thought Hitler a good egg. The game which brought him fame must have cropped up in their lengthy chat. C.B. Fry explaining cricket to the Führer in the Reichschancellery requires Tom Stoppard at his best.

The autobiography had an infelicitous publication date: 1939. Shortly people were wanting to intern CB in the Isle of Man with the Italian waiters and German professors. He also visited Hollywood, where he met C. Aubrey Smith (naturally) and P.G. Wodehouse (another Hitler fan) and Boris Karloff, who CB decided made a good monster because he understood the type, which included Zeus on Olympus. Nonsense! Boris (real name Bill Pratt) told me at the Oval that he was laying railroad track for a living; the line finished at Hollywood, so he decided to become an actor.

HOBBS UND SUTCLIFFE!

CB ended reciting in bed ball-by-ball commentaries of cricket battles long ago.

He and Beatrice died and so in 1968 did *Mercury*.

He was as Churchill described Russia, a riddle wrapped in a mystery inside an enigma. He was F.E. Smith's better at Oxford, and became, to Lord Beaverbrook anyway, 'the cleverest man in the Kingdom'. Yet he never achieved even a committee seat at Lord's. As Churchill's enemies whispered, there was a fatal flaw in the metal.

He suffered from nervous trouble, admitting him to hospitals which in those days unashamedly bore the lovely name 'asylum'. Distant diagnosis is difficult, but his was possibly manic-depressive illness, swinging him from easy-going charm to suicidal despair. We all have our pendulum. It can swing gently like the hall clock, but also like a ball on a crane, demolishing the personality.

There is no more stigma in a mental illness than in a physical one. Talleyrand and Byron both honourably bore a club foot. F.E. Smith had his quirks – there was that girl on the Battersea Park bench. But had FE instead of CB suffered the psychiatric condition, nobody would have heard of him at all. He couldn't play cricket.

References:

Fry, C.B.: *Life Worth Living*, London, 1939
Gordon, R.: *Fifty Years a Cricketer*, London, 1986
Morris, R.: *The Captain's Lady*, London, 1985
Swanton, E.W.: *As I Said at the Time*, London, 1983
The Dictionary of National Biography 1951-1960, Oxford, 1971

Style

ALAN ROSS

ALTHOUGH MOST PEOPLE would agree on what constitutes 'style' in cricket, it remains a subjective judgment, and difficult to define. Is it inextricably linked with good looks and/or graceful movement, so that it would be impossible for an unattractive man to be an attractive batsman? The term 'a beautiful mover' has been applied to many fielders, but when it was applied in the 1950s to Willie Watson, a golden-haired former footballer and fine cover-point (who once heroically saved a Lord's Test with Trevor Bailey against Australia) it used to irritate Alec Bedser. Either you stop the ball or you don't, Alec would grumble. No-one ever accused him of being a beautiful mover, yet there were few nobler sights at the time than Bedser running up to bowl, left arm reaching for the sky and hips pivoting.

When I first began to watch county cricket in the mid-1930s my favourite players – those to whom I was drawn by something more than solid worth – were all 'stylists', elegant in technique and willowy of figure. Two played for Sussex: Alan Melville and K.S. Duleepsinhji; and high among others were C.F. Walters of Worcestershire and Mushtaq Ali of India. They were, all four of them, masters of the very late-cut and the leg-glance, to an extent that these strokes, no longer an important part of the modern batsman's repertoire, came in my mind to be associated with the very notion of beauty in batsmanship. When I came to write about Ranji more recently, I discovered that it was his addiction to and control over these strokes that singled him out from even the greatest of his contemporaries.

What was the charm of the late-cut and the glance to an adolescent schoolboy? Ranji saw the value of the late-cut and the leg-glance in the fact that they made use of the ball's velocity and direction, merely deflecting its course and helping it on its way. I can still remember the physical thrill of watching Melville's caressive steer of the ball through the slips or off his legs, the bat's contact being of the sheerest and the sound negligible. If there was music in stroke play, it was here. Later Melville came to captain South Africa and to compose a string of austerely-made Test centuries, but there were few cuts and glances in them, and for me the old magic had gone.

There have been stylish players since – Tom Graveney and David Gower, for example – but none quite so exquisite in my eyes. It is also a fact, of course, that a batsman can have more style than substance. Two of Australia's most elegant post-war batsmen were Graeme Hole and Paul Sheahan, the former with a backlift even higher than Peter May's. Frank Tyson put a cruel end to his career, and Sheahan's runs never quite compared with the manner of their compiling.

Was Leonard Hutton the most complete master of the classical style? Certainly he never made an awkward or aesthetically unpleasing movement, his technique a refinement of economy and timing. Whereas in Hutton's case, as in Graveney's and Gower's, one was conscious of grace rather than strength, an innings by May or Dexter made one equally aware of power. Colin Cowdrey was the most courteous of batsmen, all timing and no coercion, but could one call him a stylist? If not, does it simply come down to a matter of build?

There have always been cricketers with a certain narcissistic quality to them, who bat as if looking into a mirror, their posture held just that second longer than absolutely necessary. Equally there are fine players who have no great presence at the wicket, their accumulation of runs always slightly surprising to the onlooker. You can overlook Waugh's presence except when he is in the act of scoring, whereas Dean Jones imposes himself from the moment he goes out to bat. Greg Chappell was a batsman of the purest gifts, but never flamboyant, no maker of visual images.

A lack of apparent effort, a coolness of approach, seem to be ingredients of style; but they cannot be the only ingredients, otherwise Gower would be out on his own. These are characteristics he shared with Frank Worrell, the most graceful among West Indian batsmen as well as the most languid of movers. Where Weekes and Walcott in their different ways, and reflecting their different statures, epitomised purpose and strength, Worrell often looked as if he might fall asleep at the wicket. As graceful, in a way more reminiscent of Walters or Melville, was Jeffrey Stollmeyer, a Trinidad and West Indies opening batsman of charm and accomplishment, with an equal predilection for the glance and the cut. Tragically, he died last year, the victim of an armed robbery.

It would appear that figure and deportment are relevant to style, for it is hard to think of a squat batsman, however good, who qualifies. Ranji was not tall, but, in his youth, very slim. George Cox was a self-consciously stylish player, his manner of leaving a ball outside the off stump as eloquent as his cover drive. He, too, was not tall, but he was beautifully made, and at cover-point moved as silkily over the turf as Watson. Power and style are not inimical to each other, but whereas in Hammond the power element predominated, his Gloucestershire colleague Barnett was stylish to the point of recklessness.

There are romantic cricketers as well as stylish ones: Keith Miller and Denis Compton, for example, both chivalrous to a degree and lavish in their sense of fun. Neither was exactly stylish in the Duleepsinhji/Gower sense, nor could this be said of batsmen like Kanhai and Milburn, though these last two displayed a physical exuberance that put them into a category of their own.

Is style the prerogative of batsmen? Or would the lovely approach to the wicket of Lindwall qualify him, in a way that Trueman, equally handsome of action, would be denied by an earthbound stockiness? Yet there have been bowlers galore who have been a delight to watch simply by reason of their grace, like Verity or Peebles among slower bowlers, Hadlee, Larwood and Hammond among quicker. I used to think it very stylish when Jardine, E.R.T. Holmes and Freddie Brown, among others, wore a silk handkerchief knotted at the neck; so perhaps a certain dandyism is yet another necessary element.

Whatever it is about 'style' in a cricketer, I think, whether consciously or not, we all recognise it when we see it.

Cricket on Elysian Fields

JOHN HOLMSTROM

WESLEY HALL TURNS in the far distance, ducks his head and begins to steam in towards us, the small gold cross bucking on his brown chest. Thank God he's not the force he once was – no longer bowling at ninety m.p.h. – but the sight is still awesome, especially when you're down to your eighth wicket and need twenty-three more runs to record your first ever victory over the West Indies.

With a hiss and a powerful thump (echoed in the batsman's heart) Hall reaches the crease and bowls a skimming away-swinger. Billy Palmer, saintly poisoner, sets his feet and thwacks the ball away to the third-man boundary. His confidence is growing, he having carefully steadied the Elysian boat after a brilliant run-a-minute partnership between Carl Philipp Emanuel Bach and André Masséna had finally run aground on the Prince of Essling's impulsiveness: one does not attempt runs like that to an apparent misfield by Gary Sobers.

Shifty Murtlock had followed almost at once, and then Bach perished on 92, wafting airily outside his off stump with only the most token fidget of the feet. Richard Crashaw had crashed two loose balls, then nose-dived; Cyril Tourneur – author of *The Revenger's Tragedy* and no relation to Yorkshire's much-loved Cyril Turner – found Lance Gibbs more than his match as a twister.

Sobers is now recalled, troubling Isaac Watts with some lazy floaters. But Watts, who emerged on India's coral strand last winter as a subtle medium-pace schemer who could bat a bit (two dour fifties against state sides), is not about to give his wicket away. Slack-wristed, he steers neat singles to give Palmer the bowling. By the time Charlie Griffith relieves Hall at the Pavilion End, we are 278 for eight and only nine runs divide us from victory. Then a quick off-cutter from Sobers deceives Watts and catches the shoulder of his bat. Gibbs claims him in the gulley.

Von Eschscholtz had kept wicket neatly enough on his Test debut, but showed little sign of batting intelligence at this level. A lucky snick gets him to the other end, where Palmer picks a shorter ball from Sobers and lofts it grandly towards the mid-on boundary, clearing Seymour Nurse and beating Basil Butcher's race to cut it off. Then – horror of horrors – the poisoner changes his mind too late from an obvious attempt to repeat the dose, and plays on. Our last two batsmen are left to get the remaining five runs.

Eschscholtz glances Griffith to leg for a single. Griffith softens up emblematic Francis Quarles with a ball rising towards the chin. Quarles ducks, just in time. The next delivery, rising a shade lower, catches him between two minds. Involuntarily the poor pietist raises a bat to protect himself. The ball knocks aside his right glove – and ricochets off his helmet, high and wide enough to evade Hendriks's salmon-like leap behind the stumps. Michael Carew hurtles round the boundary from long-leg. Too late! The ball lollops across the line. For the first time, however shakily, Elysium have defeated the West Indies.

This match, you'll be amazed to hear, took place only on the astral plane, between a West Indies side of the late 1960s and one drawn from a wholly fictitious Elysian League made up largely of teams of non-cricketers who have somehow (by cloning, brainwashing and tireless astral aerobics) been transformed into talented players. It's a complex and sophisticated evolution from the Dab Cricket of one's schooldays, where – stabbing blindly with a pencil on to an open book – the letters you landed on represented runs, maiden balls or wickets according to their rarity value. The next step was a squared chart (maths paper) with perhaps two thirds of the squares blank and the rest representing runs or chances of wickets, these depending probably on the respective skills of the batsman and bowler involved, the outcome decided by reference to a further chart or the roll of dice.

This kind of fantasy game, as one grew older, remained satisfying only by dint of increasing elaboration, making it conform as nearly as possible to the vicissitudes of real-life cricket. Players would be 'graded' by various means, so that the higher-rated bowlers presented a greater threat, while the better batsmen had more chance both of resisting the 'strike balls' and of successfully and more or less consistently scoring runs. One tinkered incessantly with the grades and charts until the players' performances were reflected in the kind of averages expected of them.

Yet always, despite one's best endeavours, certain favoured players obstinately refused to thrive, while a few unfavoured ones mysteriously prospered. After a reasonable stretch of success or failure, in any well-run league, their grades would be revised to reflect this inexplicable trend. Whereupon, no less inexplicably, the 'promoted' would sometimes do less well or the 'demoted' curiously better. There could be no doubt whatever that hidden forces were at work, and it was not unknown, amid the mounting excitement, for a cold shiver to run up the spine.

The arrival of computers has now led to the development of various electronic cricket games which can be played out with cassette programs via a keyboard and a computer screen. These are usually so simplistic as to be scarcely worth bothering with, and involve a lot of tiny humanoid figures scuttling around the screen in the frenetic manner beloved of video arcades, and the cricketing equivalents of Wham! and Splat! befouling the electronic greensward.

More serious computer attempts to replicate 'real' cricket have been made for some years now. Perhaps the best – still evolving and far from perfect, but full of charm and surprises – is the brainchild of Gordon Vince, the brilliant young mathematician who devised the Deloitte 'World Ratings.' (These show not the career averages of Test players but their current standing in terms of *recent* Test performances. The further back the performance, the less it counts towards the current rating. The conditions and the quality of the opposition are also taken into account. It is a very beautiful system, and Vince has now worked out a similar one for English county players.)

His computer program for a cricket game is equally beautiful. You pick two teams of cricketers – real or imagined, past or present – and grade them for batting, bowling and fielding prowess. Batsmen's and bowlers' grades correspond roughly to the kind of average you would expect them to end with. (It would be very boring if this expectation were always to be fulfilled, but don't worry: over a shortish period like a whole season it very seldom is.)

You then feed the names and gradings into the computer, decide whether you want a three-day or a five-day match and whether you want full ball-by-ball commentary or just scorecards for each innings. You also have the option to print out what appears on the screen – essential if you're playing the 'short' (scorecards-only) version, and want to go away and do other things while the match is playing itself. The printer acquires the excitement of an old-style ticker-tape machine: dispatches from the front.

Now you add a 'seed' number of your own choice to generate the random factor which determines the game's course – then press the relevant button. Up on the screen come the names of your teams, the condition of the wicket, which captain has won the toss and who is to bat first.

In a moment the screen changes and the first innings begins. You are shown seven columns, which fill up one line (one over) at a time: time of day, bowler, batsman 1, batsman 2, overs bowled, aggregate, wickets down. A series of dots (maiden balls), figures (runs) and occasionally letters (wickets or extras) begin to appear, the batsmen changing ends with odd-number scores as well as at the end of overs. Individual batsmen's scores are given only at the end of a page or at the fall of a wicket, until the innings ends and the scorecard is shown, complete with innings analysis and bowlers' figures. Then the other side's innings starts.

In the course of the game bowlers will be changed automatically, according to the situation and their degree of freshness. Batsmen will grow in confidence the longer they stay in, and be less likely to get out. (Unseen, the computer continually calculates the balance of power of each batsman against each bowler.) In a tight spot, batsmen will graft and the scoring rate will drop; but in a run chase, or when they're well on top, the rate accelerates. Night watchmen may be sent in towards close of play. A captain will decide to enforce (or occasionally not to) the follow-on. Wickets can become more or less difficult, there can be huge partnerships or shameful collapses. All human life is there.

A further dimension is that the grading of players is adjustable. You must follow and reinforce the workings of blind chance, otherwise mathematics will always triumph in the end and those you have given the best grades will invariably end with the highest averages. The fascination lies in adjusting the grades once or twice a season, gradually raising those who have performed better than expected and lowering the disappointing ones. Heroes can be observed to decline mysteriously, and new stars rise from obscurity. It's like watching the development of real players.

The beauty of the computer game is its mystery. You feed the personalities and their various talents into the machine, then stand back and watch as news begins to arrive as if from another planet. The excitement can be breathless, but there's nothing you can do to help the players.

If you want participation, on the other hand, you need another kind of game. There was a time when almost every schoolboy could have offered some variety of 'paper cricket', conducted by blind dabbings onto charts or books. But these were in general painfully rudimentary, with none of the choices and subtleties of real life. A tail-end bat was as likely to make a big score as an opener, and all bowlers did equally well or badly.

Acute minds chafed at these inadequacies, and invented ways of refining, differentiating and elaborating a game of crude chance. In his teens the Shakespearean director John Barton ran a private league (part of an entire Ruritanian realm of his imagination) which depended on an armful of charts, lovingly stratified in several colours of ink. These took in not only the routine vicissitudes of first-class cricket but every complexion of weather – plus less common events like earthquake, riot, galloping fuserium, fast bowler dislocating knee, batsman being bitten by rabid hedgehog or umpire succumbing to bubonic plague.

In a Japanese prisoner-of-war camp – classic setting for a timeless test of British grit and imagination – the writer Denis Castle dreamed up an ingenious cricket game using two packs of playing cards shuffled together. Certain cards were to represent 'threats' if dealt from the bowler's hand, but 'parrying' (threat-nullifying) or scoring shots if produced from the batsman's hand of six laid out in front of him. Both batsmen and bowlers are graded, with the batsman advancing to higher grades as his innings matures, and thus able to claim more cards for his defence. The batsman's hand is replenished at the end of each over, but if he runs out of defensive cards and is unable to parry a bowler's attacking card, he is out.

Castle's game has been further elaborated by the bookseller and bibliographer Timothy d'Arch Smith, into a thing of extraordinary subtlety and realism where the captain of each side has to make continual decisions on behalf of his players. Does he persist with a successful fast bowler although he is tiring and has gone down a grade? Should a batsman stripped of defensive cards accept a single off the last ball but one of an over – but then have to face the next one, perhaps still without a defensive card – or gamble on the bowler's not producing a 'strike' card for the one ball left? Should he speed up the scoring rate by using defensive cards as attackers, scoring boundaries but perhaps leaving his hand dangerously weak unless the replenishments work out to his advantage? Decisions, decisions; pressures, pressures. Emotions round the table can run alarmingly high, and there is rich scope for dispute over interpretation of the rules.

It's not a quick game, though – it takes nearly half the real-life time, so you couldn't run a whole league by the playing card method, unless you had a few free years with nothing else to do. But without a league you can hardly produce a Test team to pit against the great cricketing countries. It's best to play the bulk of your league on the computer (scorecard-only version, printed out) and just a few selected matches by the playing card method. You can plan a season's fixture list in advance, building in a visiting touring team and leaving gaps for the Test matches. You pick your Test team on the usual balance of past performance and current form – more scope for debate.

There remains the nature of the personnel, and

here it's up to you whether your teams are made up of real cricketers, present or past, historical characters or wholly invented people. In the case of real players, obviously you base their grades on their figures over a whole career or a key part of it. In the case of unreal players you simply invent their initial grade, then watch it evolve. If you mix real and unreal cricketers, you must assume that the latter have undergone a total sea-change, are now in their youthful prime, trained to concert pitch, and bounding around in white flannels. (Monty Python turned out a football team of ancient Greek philosophers, but left them in their robed, bearded and sandalled senescence. We would approach the transformation more thoroughly.)

In the league run by myself and one or two friends, the sixteen teams (useful for knockout competitions) are, for what it's worth, at present as follows:

AUSTERLITZ	(Napoleon's marshals)
CHANTREY	(Anthony Powell characters)
CHARONIANS	(famous British murderers)
DIPPERMOUTH	(American rock singers)
DUCATS	(people who played only once for England)
DUODECIMOS	(bibliographers)
EISENACH	(members of the Bach family)
EVEREST	(mountaineers)
KITEZH	(Russian romantic composers)
LINNAEANS	(botanists who have

	given their names to plants)
MALCONTENTS	(Jacobean dramatists)
QUINCUNX	(metaphysical poets)
REGENSBURG	(17th and 18th century German writers)
TALLINN	(Estonian politicians, 1919-1940)
WHITEHOUSE	(forgotten American presidents)
YATTENDON	(British hymn-writers).

Last season, the metaphysicals surprised everyone by taking the championship, followed by Austerlitz and Charonians. This year, in spite of several up-gradings, all three teams seem to be in the doldrums. Marshall Ney has stopped scattering the fielders, and neither John Donne nor Charlie Peace seems able to make the ball move any more. Kitezh are currently crippled by the demoralisation of their two leading batsmen: Tchaikovsky (unrequited passion for junior member of St Petersburg ground staff) and Mussorgsky (drink). But an Estonian seam bowler called Unt is arousing interest. New Zealand are touring, and have won the first Test by some margin.

That's cricket.

A Late Innings

IAN WALLACE

IF I ADJUST THE lens of my nostalgioscope close to its maximum range (i.e. a little over fifty years) I can clearly make out F.W. Ives, one of two Charterhouse masters responsible for guiding the History 6th into the intellectual territory where one or two of our small group might pick up a scholarship or an exhibition to Oxford or Cambridge (the word Oxbridge being unknown in those days). One or two did, but I was not among them, and Freddie Ives would have needed treatment for shock if I had been.

Often in English Literature periods he would read aloud Victorian narrative poems such as 'Sohrab and Rustum' and 'The Pied Piper of Hamelin'. Although on OTC afternoons he could look vinegary and stern in his major's uniform with field boots shining like glass, he was a different proposition in sports jacket and flannels, clasping a copy of Browning as he walked up and down in front of his desk, and it was not unknown for him to brush away a tear at the beauty of the verse as the sun streamed in through the window. At times even the philistines among us were temporarily more engrossed in the fate of those Victorian heroes than in the prospect of a net later in the afternoon.

It was he who introduced us to the hilarious account of a village cricket match in A.G. Macdonnell's book *England, Their England*, an unexpected draught of sparkling irreverence about something that was taken very seriously in schools like Charterhouse before the war. For me it was another element in my burgeoning love affair with the game. Here was a shining example of how cricket could inspire prose of the highest order. It was suddenly something to read about as well as to play.

I was already familiar with another kind of cricket reading. It might surprise those under sixty to know that during a Test match against Australia before the war the front pages of the evening papers, and often those of the popular dailies as well, were entirely devoted to news and pictures of the match. There was one famous headline 'Bradman Fails'. It was a great compliment: he'd made 46. At Charterhouse, where none of us possessed a radio – portables in those days were small, heavy, expensive suitcases, far beyond a schoolboy's pocket – the communal *Daily Mirror* was fought over after breakfast as the only source of news of yesterday's play, but at least the score card was in bold type, legible from the back of the scrimmage.

I was often drawn after morning school on Saturdays

to watch the school 1st XI playing the last half hour or so before lunch. The opposition would be club sides with exotic names like I Zingari, Butterflies, Grasshoppers or the formidable and glamorous MCC, as well as other schools – Eton, Harrow, Westminster and so on. On one occasion the redoubtable G.O. Allen was in the MCC side and opened the bowling off a run that took him almost to the sight-screen, while to say that the wicket keeper was standing back is something of an understatement. None of this discomposed our hero, J.M. Lomas, a batsman of enormous talent, the peak of his light pink cap shading his features from the glare. How many he made that day I can't recall, but it was certainly a significant contribution. Had he not died young and tragically he would surely have played for England; but in fairness to a wise and splendid cricketing knight I should add that nothing remotely resembling a bouncer was bowled. It was a demonstration of what was deemed to be good fast bowling in those days: on a length and impeccably accurate.

On one unforgettable late afternoon, so late that the players' shadows were grotesquely long, Charterhouse defeated Eton in a single-innings match. My nostalgioscope finds it hard to focus on scoreboards, but I think we needed to put on 20 for the last wicket. Eton's was a cherished and seldom-attained scalp, and, as news spread of a last-wicket stand slowly and agonisingly reducing the deficit, virtually the whole school was soon standing on the grass in front of Verites and Old

Chapel to witness the outcome. There's a famous song from another school that describes a similar scene, but neither we nor the Etonians would have wished to quote it. At one end was the wicket-keeper, Arthur Bean, one of nature's number elevens, who could normally be relied on not to trouble the scorer. He didn't on this occasion; but he stayed there for more than half an hour, stubbornly denying the bowler at one end, spurning possible singles so that his more talented partner could win the match. When the winning hit was struck, cheers of football proportions rang out, competing with blaring car horns, and Arthur Bean, 0 not out, was carried shoulder high from the field. Only a year or two later he was killed in action.

I cannot really account for my continuing interest in a game for which I showed a total absence of talent. Even my rather elegant late-cut was regarded by slip fielders as manna from heaven. The beautiful 1st XI cricket ground at Charterhouse was where it began, though of course I was never good enough to play there. When, many years later, cricketing friends proposed me for MCC membership and, to my joy and surprise, I was elected, I realised there was still something missing. I was still, perforce, merely a spectator, the boy with his nose pressed to the toyshop window; only now I had a better view of the delights on the other side of the glass.

Then, in my seventieth year, I was at last invited into the shop. I played my first innings at Lord's in the form of a speech to a members' winter dinner, where I was given the signal honour of sitting on the President's right. I don't think I scored many runs, but I tried to make it what the cricket writers usually describe as a bright little cameo. Anyway, I was quite ridiculously pleased to be there.

As if that was not enough, I was asked in the week of my 70th birthday to participate in a very unusual cricket match, Bertie Joel's Celebrity XI v. The Metro Club for the Blind, to be played at Seal, near Sevenoaks. Bertie Joel, a man who does a great deal of good by stealth, and works tirelessly to raise money for many charities, must be one of the oldest MCC members still playing. 'I can't play, Bertie,' I wrote back, 'but maybe I could man the PA or bring out the drinks or something.' My friend and next-door neighbour, Tony Halstead, an MCC member who *can* play cricket, was also invited. 'Ian,' he said the night before the match, 'Bertie'll expect you to have some whites to put on for the photographs, whether you're playing or not.' This struck terror into my heart. I went up to the bedroom. The white shirt I normally use for weddings would do. Trainers and light fawn socks would *have* to do. But what about trousers? The only thing in my wardrobe that remotely resembled white flannels was an old pair of shapeless, faded oatmeal lightweight slacks, the sort of thing Robert Louis Stevenson might have worn on the beach during his declining years in Samoa. I put them in the holdall, praying devoutly that Tony was wrong. The one redeeming feature was a white sweater recently given to me, with a small logo on the front bearing the words 'English Sinfonia'.

I decided that my blazer with the golf club badge would strike a false note, but if I wore my stylish panama with its Old Carthusian ribbon, my trousers and trainers might with luck go unnoticed.

We had to arrive early for security reasons. HM the Queen was opening a new wing of Dorton House College, where the match was taking place. Not, of course, that it would affect us. The Queen would have come and gone before we started. After we'd parked the car, Tony and I were directed to a huge marquee, where we queued for coffee. As we stood in line a large and familiar figure in a voluminous lounge suit made his way towards us carrying a cricket bag so full that the bat handle protruded like the bowsprit of a brigantine. It was Patrick Moore. 'We'd better get changed,' he said. 'Bertie's gone already.' It was about 10.30 a.m., and the match was not due to start until two o'clock. 'What's the hurry?' we asked.

'Photographs and presentations,' he said laconically, and was gone. 'That won't include me, I'm not playing,' I said to Tony. At that moment I was handed a list of those to be presented. My name was on it. I thought of the oatmeal slacks and the logo on my sweater and wanted to go home.

On the way to the dressing room I noticed that everyone else had very professional looking cricket bags. One of the cricketers smiled at me and said 'I'm

Dennis Amiss. Delighted to meet you.' What had I let myself in for?

Carrying my panama I walked through crowds of spectators to the new wing, where the presentations would take place. All the other cricketers, including Bertie, were in blazers. I walked between Patrick Moore and Colin Moynihan, the Minister for Sport, who had gallantly come down to encourage us, which made it impossible not to be noticed. I had seriously underestimated the importance of the occasion. Fortunately there were a great many people in the large room, including my friend Brian Johnston, who was officiating. He looked at me, a smile flickering on his lips, but tactfully made no comment. It was soon obvious that Her Majesty could not possibly shake hands with everyone, particularly those of us near the back of the queue; so as we were being politely shepherded through the door back into the sunshine by an equerry, and I was congratulating myself on avoiding an embarrassing moment, the Duke of Edinburgh and his party, who had made an unscheduled detour, were heading straight for us. We fell back in confusion, but he was still forced to stop, and decided to shake a few hands himself. I heard someone call my name. He shook my hand and, for a few seconds, took in my rotund figure and singularly inappropriate choice of apparel. Thankfully, he decided that it was not a moment for small talk.

I had not realised that the Metro Club for the blind play cricket with a ball the size of a football, which has something like ball bearings or a tiny bell inside it

BIG DEAL... PRESENTED TO
THE ROYAL CORGI!
VIP
ENCL

so that it rattles and tinkles when it bounces. When a totally blind batsman is at the crease the bowler must ensure that the ball bounces twice before reaching the batsman, and must ask him if he is ready before bowling. He must then shout 'Play!' as he releases the ball. For a partially-sighted player the ball need only bounce once, and of course the blind batsmen have a runner. Any ball that the umpire judges unreachable by the batsman is a wide. Blind batsmen cannot be out LBW, and there are eight balls to the over. Other than that the normal laws apply. When the Metros are fielding the blind fielders can catch the opposing batsmen first bounce.

I was looking forward to watching, from the comfort of the pavilion, how Dennis Amiss and the former West Indies Test star from Jamaica, Reg Scarlett, coped with this heavy and unwieldy ball when Bertie asked if I would mind umpiring. The last time I had umpired had been when I was fifteen. It was a 25-over match and, apart from a miscount of the number of overs, my decisions were accepted without demur. The Metros were batting, which put me in the eminently satisfying position of calling wides and no-balls when Amiss and Scarlett were bowling; what's more they both sportingly agreed with me. Even with that degree of friendliness and sportsmanship, I got a glimmer of an impression of the strain and concentration attached to the job of an umpire. I was too tired to stand for the other innings, and retired to a deck chair with a cup of tea. The keenness of the Metros' batting had been a revelation, and the capacity of the blind players to pick up the flight of the ball and hit it on the second or third attempt was impressive.

When our XI batted it soon became clear why the Metros have such a high success record. There were five blind players in the side, and they stood as close, and closer, to the bat, all through the innings, as the Pakistanis do to tail-enders when Qadir is bowling in a Test match. The partially-sighted attack was good and, in fairness to our side, accustomed to the ball. At first they tied everyone up in knots and wickets began to fall. A young Indian sitting near me remarked 'I think they're going to beat us.' In the end, despite some spirited batting by Dennis Amiss and others, including a brief, grafting innings from Moore, P., they did, and it was in no small part because of the courage and application of those ever-vigilant blind close fielders, who made defensive strokes suicidal and who, my replacement umpire told me afterwards, counted every ball and constantly wanted an update on the score.

The deck chair conversation among the knot of dismissed batsmen and those awaiting their fate was relaxed and illuminating. A very senior and long-standing club cricketer was telling of a ground in Hertfordshire where on sunny evenings all the overs have to be bowled from one end for a while, as the sun setting behind the bowler's arm makes it impossible to see the ball at the other. He told also how he had broken many bats hitting yorkers for four. He described a visit, light years ago, to Jack Hobbs's shop in the city, where the great man offered to replace free any Jack Hobbs bat that he broke during the season. 'I broke three,' he said, 'and when I took the second one in he told me he'd go broke if he replaced it for nothing. I didn't blame him,' he added magnanimously.

Somebody asked me about *My Music*, the radio panel game (formerly on TV) in which I'd been a panel member for twenty-three years, and the conversation turned to the question in which we are required to suggest signature tunes for different occupations. I told them that I had been rebuked by Frank Muir for being vulgar in this sort of thing, quoting as an example the time when we were asked to supply a signature tune for doctors. I had said I could only think of one for a very young doctor, who was an enthusiastic member of the local light operatic society. Sounding the chest of a well-endowed girl with bronchitis he might have thrown down his stethoscope, I suggested, and burst into 'The hills are alive . . .' As the laughter subsided our young Indian cricketer could be heard completing the line for me – '. . . with the sound of mucus . . .'

On the way home Tony and I didn't talk much. We were too tired. I lay back in the passenger seat and closed my eyes. Maybe, I thought to myself, just in case, I'd better buy some white flannels and socks; and perhaps I'll take the golf club badge off the blazer – I don't play golf any more, after all. But I think I'll leave the English Sinfonia logo on my sweater. If nothing else, it inspires thoughts of a Floral Dance XI – fiddle, cello, big bass drum, bassoon, flute and euphonium. I bet they wouldn't stand a chance against the Metros, either.

The Use of Memory

TREVOR McDONALD

IF YOUR ATTACHMENT to a game is as good as the people who induct you into its intricate rites, I was singularly fortunate in my associates. In a lifelong affair with the summer game, I have met some of the finest and most influential cricketers in history. To them I owe the constant stirrings of a deep smouldering passion, and, to borrow from Wordsworth

in hours of weariness sensations sweet,
felt in the blood and felt along the heart.

When my mother lost the battle to make me spend more time at my books than on the rough and unprepared strips on which I unsuccessfully tried to master the craft, she gave in gracefully; and to show goodwill, she introduced me to Learie Constantine. He was a distant family acquaintance; I was overawed, but too young to sit usefully at the feet of the great man. I was fortunate to meet him again many years later.

Great players are often *not* great teachers. Constantine was both. He had not only played the game with consummate skill, he had thought deeply about it, and in the evening of his years he was a glorious benefactor to any eager supplicant.

He was always illuminating on the art of slip fielding. He would analyse where the slip fielders stood in relation to each other, how they prepared themselves as the bowler approached; and how wicket keepers developed an understanding between their job and that of their neighbour at nearby first slip.

Constantine's humanity, his concern for the art and its practitioners made him a fallible genius. And such was the quality of his brilliance that what we, his underlings, unkindly remembered most clearly those rare occasions on which he read a situation wrongly.

When Nari Contractor captained India in the West Indies in the early 1960s, Gary Sobers had begun playing Sheffield Shield Cricket in Australia. He'd made the mind-numbing aeroplane dash from Melbourne to Port of Spain for the start of the Trinidad Test, arriving only on the morning of the first day. It was heady, dramatic stuff, but it persuaded Constantine to sound a note of caution. Observing that Sobers, who in the course of doing everything in the game with maddening skill, was also a great slip catcher, Constantine suggested that perhaps Captain Frank Worrell might be advised *not* to put Sobers in that position at the start of the Test, since – and I remember his words – 'he's still in the air'.

The game began, and we sat perched on the edge of our seats in the commentary box, as Sobers went to first slip. A portent of West Indian disaster hung heavily in the air. Charlie Griffiths, later to be accused by the Indian tour management of employing 'terror tactics' steamed in to bowl to Contractor. With very few Indian runs on the board, the Indian captain attempted to fend off a ball of incredible pace and one which rose menacingly off a good length. It went off the bat and flew into the slips, higher than head height, with the speed of lightning. Sobers climbed into the air, clutched the ball in both hands and fell to the ground with his quarry safely pressed against his chest. The partisan crowd erupted and we, who had caught a glimpse of that rare phenomenon, Learie Constantine's fallibility, looked at each other and smiled, never daring to snigger in the presence of the great man.

Constantine loved bowling in his day, and his approach to that department of the game was rigidly tactical. He could spot a batsman's failings a mile away, suggest just how he could be prised out – and was hardly ever wrong about that. He made me aware of the virtue of keeping the ball well up, although in his day, he was not averse to employing the occasional short-pitched delivery; and he was one of the few quick bowlers who studied and really appreciated the art of good spin-bowling. Batting, though, was his love. His philosophy here was quintessentially West Indian. He believed that the ball was there to be hit as hard and as often as possible. He was the great improviser of shots;

his one priority seemed to be getting the ball out of the ground. He was, it almost follows, impatient at craven, defensive play, although he knew it had its place. He preferred the hitters. To sit with Learie Constantine while Weekes, Walcott, Sobers, Kanhai, Nurse or Butcher was in full flow, was to add a new and lofty dimension to an age-old joy. His insight augmented and improved the strokeplay. His love of the game, acquired early and shaped in the testing crucible of the English league, shone like a well directed beam of light.

I am indebted to Learie for reasons other than those which have to do with cricket. In 1962 I was sent to London from Port of Spain to report on Trinidad's Independence Conference at Marlborough House. The communiqué at the end of each day's session could easily be summarised in half a dozen short sentences. My predicament was that I was supposed to produce a *ten*-minute report every evening. India were that season's tourists in England, and I would make my way every morning to Learie's hotel, where we would begin by watching the cricket. The mood induced by our watching and talking about the play was so warm, that he could be persuaded to tell tales about what actually went on at Malborough House, without ever losing touch with India's struggle against England.

More than anything else, though, Learie Constantine had a magical memory. Ask him about a game in 1930, and he would turn his eyes heavenwards, and with that lovely lilting voice he would say; 'Patsy Hendren was standing at first slip. There were three other men close to bat as I took my guard . . .'

His friend C.L.R. James wrote of his batting:

> Constantine's leg-glance from outside the off-stump to long leg was a classical stroke. It was not due to his marvellous West Indian eyes and wrists. It was due, if you must have it, to his marvellous West Indian brains. He saw that the best League bowlers were always out to pin him down, and the conditions, including the marvellous league crowds, compelled him to work out new and safe ways of countering them.

In his autobiography C.B. Fry said of Learie:

> One could understand why his name became first on the list of all Lancashire League cricketers. In this class of cricket, where matches are decided in one afternoon, I cannot envisage a player with better qualifications. In a quarter of an hour of terrific speed bowling or unorthodox hitting he could swing the fortunes of a match.

Frank Worrell, the West Indian star forced to languish in the shadows of those who merited less the captaincy of the West Indies, used his time, not to sulk, but to refine his knowledge of the way the West Indies could channel their skills into playing to win.

I met him just before he took the West Indies to Australia for that consistently glorious 1960-61 series which included the famous Brisbane tie. How would he approach his job as skipper, I had enquired over a glass of beer late one evening in a Port of Spain nightclub.

With a soft smile in his eyes, he chuckled quietly and said: 'Teamwork.'

Later I heard more of the story. On the journey to Australia, Frank arranged to have the new members of the squad seated next to the more seasoned players. He made himself constantly available to the newer players. The talking, the encouragement, the building of team spirit had begun.

Frank was probably the most gracious person in a game populated by many gentlemen. His small personal acts of kindness were made even in the heat of the fiercest battle. The Australian spinner Lindsay Kline remembers walking out to bat in the punishingly nerve-racking final minutes of the tied Test in Brisbane, Frank slapping him on the back and wishing him good luck. People were important to Worrell. Kline remembers because his mouth framed a response, but it was never heard. Crippling fear consumed his words.

Wes Hall remembers preparing to deliver the last few balls of the match, when the runs required matched the number of deliveries to come, one for one. Wes sought the advice of the oracle. 'What shall I bowl, skip?' he enquired. Frank's famous reply: 'Whatever you do Wes, don't for God's sake bowl no-ball.'

Was it any wonder that at the end of that famous tour, described so memorably by the late 'Johnny' Moyes, half a million people choked the streets of Melbourne, not for an open air pop concert, but simply to say goodbye to Frank Worrell and the team he had so superbly moulded? The crowds threw ticker tape at their open cars, pleading through a thousand banners 'Come back soon.' Worrell, with the Australian captain at the time, Richie Benaud, had pioneered a new spirit in Test cricket, and the people of Australia had shown their appreciation in full measure.

In everything he did, Frank Worrell was a man of immense generosity. He would give items of his cricket kit to students and to poor children, and he never sought any publicity for so doing. On the all too few occasions on which we met he gave me his time freely.

I was born too late to meet George Headley, the best captain the West Indies never had, and much, much too late, to meet the Trinidadian batsman W.H. St Hill, who played with such ease, flicking the ball away like a conjuror. It was said of him that no-one batting at the other end could have overshadowed him. He saw the ball early. He played it as late as anyone. In 1928 *The Times* correspondent said of him:

> W.H. St Hill, can be relied upon to provide entertainment in the West Indies side.
>
> He is very supple, has a beautifully erect stance and having lifted his bat, performs amazing apparently double-jointed tricks with his wrists and arms. Some of those contortions are graceful and remunerative, such as his gliding to leg, but some are unsound and dangerous, such as the exaggerated turn of the wrist in cutting. He will certainly play some big and attractive innings, but some others may be easily curtailed by his exotic fancy in dealing with balls on the off side.

How I would have loved to talk to St Hill about the art of batsmanship; how wonderful it would have been to see the greatness of Headley.

But I saw Sobers, Walcott, Kanhai, Weekes, Richards and Lloyd among others, and what's more I knew and talked to Constantine and Worrell.

And the memories are warm. T.S. Eliot says

This is the use of memory:
For liberation – not less of love but expanding
Of love beyond desire, and so liberation
From the future as well the past.

I seek no liberation from the memories of cricketing friends.

Bob Caught Carol Bowled Alice

MARK LAWSON

OTHER MEN PERHAPS visualised whips, willing women and unlikely physical contortions but, for Graham Sterling, the fantasy life which most mattered, with which he would distract himself at times of personal dissatisfaction, was as an England batsman. Whatever the women's magazines said, this was probably true of most men of his age and background, which was unpushy middle-class.

Only the details of the dream had altered over time. In adolescence he had projected himself as a tall, lean stroke-maker in an old-fashioned blue cap, perhaps even tasselled, hooking and driving a perspiring Australian fast bowler before raising a bat in casual acknowledgement of the expected century. He was thirty now – the age at which real sportsmen began to contemplate retirement – and the picture had changed. Now he was a chunky tail-ender, his head wet with terror inside the maximum-security hamster-cage of a helmet, prodding bravely at the racing sphere, making a plucky fifty, doing – and this was the point – better than anyone expected. Sometimes he wondered if this was representative of a change in the terms on which he met life.

In the passenger seat of the car on that Saturday morning, heading for Devon, he had just edged a four over the slips off one of the quickest fast bowlers the West Indies had ever produced. The crowd was rising to him, flapping banners full of affectionate puns about the dependability of English Sterling.

He opened his eyes. They were in the fast lane, the distances to Devon on the road signs reducing by even numbers like the scoreboard total of runs required to win a match. The noise of a cricket crowd, which had served as the soundtrack for his fantasy, was coming from the radio. This was reality's version of England v West Indies, curiously omitting G.P. Sterling from the team-sheet.

He tried to listen but, for the second time on the journey, the radio reception had become so poor – Eliza, who knew everything, announced exactly which range of hills would be responsible – that Jeff and Graham could no longer tell whether a sudden boiling-up of noise was static, the crowd's reaction to another six crashed by a West Indian batsman or (an unlikely occurrence, admittedly) the fall of a visitor's wicket.

'Could you, er, pull up for, er, er, a minute, just while we get the score, if it's not . . .', said Graham to Eliza, his wife, who was driving. The successful conduction of a Japanese car between West London, where they lived, and the coast of Devon, where they were heading for a bank holiday weekend, was one of the many activities in which Eliza now doubted Graham's competence. This aspect of their marriage also accounted for the tentative nature of his request.

'Go on, Lizzy, be a sport,' urged Jeff, in a manner which was equally typical.

Eliza smiled, as she had not when Graham asked, and directed her voice towards the back seat where Jeff was seated with Susan, whose husband he was.

'Well, Sue,' Eliza wondered, 'should we let the boys have their way?'

'Mmmmm, they've been quite good so far,' replied Susan, entering with ease into the frequent English game – played socially, sexually and in business – of recasting adults as children. Was it nostalgia for the over-quoted innocence and protectedness of childhood, or for its quiet spite and secrets and the newness of the body's pulses?

The boys were, on this occasion, humoured, and Eliza pulled onto the hard shoulder of the motorway.

'Be quick,' she said, her mock-mummy voice still on, 'this is strictly only for emergencies.'

'This is an emergency,' grinned Jeff, winning a smile from Eliza which Graham suspectd he would not have got for the same line. But then, he reflected, he was equally unlikely to have thought of it.

Graham fumbled quickly through the wavelengths,

searching for a piece of the ether where the news from Lord's would come through clearer. Broken pieces of speech – 'the Home Secretary . . . Lloyd-Webber . . . sewage . . . Lake Meech agreement' – and song – 'love . . . willya . . . summertime . . . love . . . dontcha' – caught their ears between stretches of instrumental music, French and German, before they settled on: 'And he hooks . . . and they'll have to send out search parties for that one! And at the end of the over West Indies are 281 for one. Trevor?'

Graham and Jeff exchanged the glances of two unacquainted mourners at a funeral. Eliza reached over, flicked the radio off and looked for a break in the stream of passing cars.

'Well, well,' she crooned. 'I wish I was there.'

'I thought you didn't like cricket,' Jeff said.

'I don't. But I do like very big black men in white clothes. I don't understand all this fuss about not letting women in the pavilion at Lord's. It's the dressing room I'd like to be in.'

Graham added to the laughter from Susan and Jeff but he always assumed himself to be the butt of such sexual banter from his wife.

It was scorching beyond the hopes of an English August – much of the conversation had involved swapping half-digested pieces of fear from articles and documentaries about the environmental crisis – and Graham's eyes were crumpled against the glare.

He pulled down the padded sun-shield, but it was of the depressing variety which has a mirror on the back, so tilted as to find the hairline of a man of average height in the front seat. Graham was no longer taking evidence from the Committee on Male Pattern Baldness, which had been investigating him since the discovery of a substance suspiciously like human hair in the plughole a few years earlier, so he snapped back the device and, making the seat-belt more comfortable around a stomach at which he declined to look down, he closed his eyes and saw that he was 42 not out and had forced the West Indian captain to bring on the spinner.

In the back seat, Susan was reading a book. It was a thin, pale novel by, the jacket photograph attested, a thin, pale female novelist about a spinster archaeologist wondering whether to go to bed with a married computer tycoon she had met at Bangkok airport. The sentence which her eyes were scanning at that moment was: '. . . and answer yes to the still, moist, urgent question at the centre of her being . . .' Jeff, who had never been seen by any of the others with any literary text except a cricket book or the Chancellor's Autumn Statement, was gazing at the cows and sheep in the speeding fields as if they were a code he might crack. Jeff was nearly six foot four and his tanned legs, shown off by clean white tennis shorts, were pushed against the back of the driver's seat. Sometimes, when she braked, Eliza could feel the pressure of them through the shielding seat and her cotton dress.

They reached their hotel, which was called Cliff's, just after the lunch interval in the Test match. As Eliza pulled into the car park Graham flicked on the radio and heard a crash and howl which seemed like interference but must have been delight as the commentator said 'And that's his double century too!' The 'too' was the real wound. He switched off as quickly as if he had just heard the beginning of a party political broadcast.

'Oh, shit!' said Jeff. 'We'll be lucky to get them out for a thousand at this rate.'

'It's only a game,' said Eliza breezily, the degree of irritation caused quite calculated, as they walked to reception to claim possession of two double rooms at the Summer Weekend Break rate.

Eliza and Graham had come to Cliff's two or three times a year since before they were married. Eliza, a language teacher who patrolled most written and spoken prose for infringements, had once pointed out to the owners, a ruddied and courteous couple, that the apostrophe in the name of the hotel was either redundant –Cliffs was adequate –or misplaced, as it must be a hotel dependent on several escarpments rather than one. 'Oh no, lovey,' said Mrs Owner (the couple's surname had been offered only once and had not stuck). 'The chap who started this place up – we bought it from him, see – was called Cliff. It's, like, a play on words.'

Eliza and Graham would often invite another couple to Cliff's but this was the first time it had been Jeff and Susan. Jeff was a junior partner in the City brokerage firm of Potomac Johnson Hodge, formed when the old English stockbrokers Hanratty Forest Hodge, for whom he had worked since university, was taken over by Potomac Johnson (Boston) Inc. He could never quite explain to the others precisely what he was paid to sit in a suit and do but Susan had confided in Eliza – 'if he knows I've told you, he'll go loopy' – that he earned £100,000 a year for performing these dark tasks satisfactorily, which was four times the salary Graham received as Assistant Press Officer in an oil company. *He* could have explained *his* duties to the others all too easily, but chose not to from some shade of shame. He edited the company magazine *Rush!* and tried to convince journalists on the telephone that his employers always put the environment first. A typical point of contrast between the two men was that Jeff had been squeezed into membership of MCC (theoretical waiting list from cradle to grave) by a senior partner.

Eliza and Graham were shown to their room by Mr Owner and Susan and Jeff by Mrs Owner. They changed – Graham wore shorts, wincing at the width of his thighs – and met on the terrace for prawn sandwiches and Chablis. From the terrace the view was past the parched grass, darkening into rock, of Cliff's (grammatically perfect) Cliff, to the beach and sea.

'Look at that!' said Jeff. 'Flat as the track at the Oval.'

'I know,' agreed Graham. 'When we were down in March it looked like a spinner's wicket in Lahore. Even I could have made the ball turn on something as rough as that.'

There was no reason why Eliza and Susan should have comprehended this arcane exchange – a metaphorical comparison between the south coast sea in different seasons and the texture of two international wickets – so they could be forgiven for changing the subject.

'Anyone coming for a paddle after lunch?' Susan wondered.

'A paddle maybe. Not a swim,' replied Eliza. 'Any stretch of water which doesn't contain the residues of my husband's employers will be thick with the excrement of our ancestors.'

'This environment business,' cut in Jeff. 'I've been thinking. How far would it have to go before it changed the nature of the game? I mean, the greater the air pollution, presumably the better it will be for seam bowlers, ball's bound to swing . . . conversely, the more rubbish, the more poison bubbling up through the earth, quids in for spinners, wouldn't it be? It might actually be possible to trace the state of the planet through the bowling averages. This is the way the world ends, not with a bang but a googly . . .'

'Sometimes I wish I understood cricket,' said Susan mildly. 'Not always but sometimes.'

'It's comparatively simple,' Eliza reassured her. 'England have been doing a bit better since all the English players who went to South Africa were replaced by all the South African players who came to England. Is that right, boys?'

Graham blushed. Jeff stuck out his tongue at Eliza

and rotated it, so that it momentarily resembled a rhubarb ice lolly being sucked.

After lunch they strolled round the tourist shops dotted on the steep road by which the hotel was reached.

'Hey, Gray,' shouted Jeff in one of them. 'Look at these.'

He was holding up a children's beach cricket set, a perspex zipper bag which held a bright yellow plastic bat of around quarter size and a red ball that would have been the perfect size for squash but barely an eighth of the weight. There were no stumps. Jeff called Eliza and Susan over.

'I know that one member of the committee will instantly vote against this proposal – yes, I'm looking at you, Lizzy – but how about a quick game on the beach? Midget equipment . . .'

'Jeff, I'm sure you're being too modest,' drawled Eliza; but she added that if it would please the boys to play they should, and – who knew? – the girls might just turn out. When the wives had moved back beyond listening distance, Jeff picked up a half-size tennis ball from another stand, which contained junior tennis rackets, and squeezed it, like someone testing fruit.

'Make a bit of a game of it,' he murmured to Graham. 'That little red thing's going to drift like a leaf.'

The unprecedented August sun, in attacking the planet, had dried and packed sand left damp by the retreating sea. 'Good, hard pitch,' Jeff remarked, repeatedly stamping a square of it like an angry child. The beach had been Cliff's personal property, a right passed on to Mr and Mrs Owner along with his hotel, and, as most of the present residents were too frail to make the descent to it, Jeff and Graham could mark out the pitch almost wherever they chose. They agreed to a short off-side boundary fixed by a litter of jagged rocks at the foot of the cliff and a substantially longer leg-side boundary designated by the breaking waves. This, Jeff solemnly pointed out, would mean that it was easier to hit leg-side fours later in the game, as the tide came in, but that was fine because it gave weight to the decision required of whoever won the toss. Each of the four would have two innings, in rotation, with the other three attempting to dismiss them, each bowling an over, also in turn. A complicated succession of tossed coins produced a batting order of Susan, Eliza, Graham, Jeff.

The wicket the batsman was defending was Eliza's blush-coloured tubular canvas bag; the bowler's stump was a wide flat pebble. Susan took guard rounders-fashion, standing upright with the bat held horizontal from her waist.

'Gray,' shouted Jeff, who seemed to have appointed himself fielding captain, 'do you want to open the bowling?'

'Well, er, if you . . .'

The other man threw him the shrunken tennis ball, waved Eliza back to the leg-side surf and himself crouched behind the overnight bag.

Graham had once taken four wickets in an Under-14 match, when the other side was chasing runs. He was an undistinguished less-than-medium pacer but Susan was a girl, so he thought he ought to give her even more of a chance than a man would have had. If a film had been taken of him running in, the viewer would have thought it was slow motion. The ball crawled through the air, Susan swung, made a contact which bent the flimsy bat concave and, as the ball dropped at her feet, dashed through for one run.

On the fourth delivery of Graham's over Susan heaved the bat and edged it in the direction of a boarded-up refreshments stall. She ran, but Jeff leapt sideways, collected the ball and hurled it at the canvas bag.

'Owzat?' he yelled.

'Come off it, darling,' gasped Susan, breathless from her dash back to regain her ground.

'Run out! Bloody run out!' Jeff shrieked. 'She was bloody yards out!'

'Look, I think, you know, if . . .' began Graham.

'Next ball,' shouted Susan, taking up her stance.

Susan made five runs off the over. Jeff decided that he would bowl the next. He stood by the bowler's pebble, rubbing the tennis ball rhythmically against his thigh. You could guess that, in his mind, he was on television. Graham took a surreptitious look at Jeff's trunks bulge. He always did this when with other men in bathing gear. An analyst might have suggested that this was submerged homosexuality but, in truth, it was neurotic heterosexuality. Graham was interested in, allowing for angles, the comparative fullness of the pouch: how much he had to worry about. Jeff turned and walked away across the beach, further and further, until he looked like a parched man in a desert in a beer commercial. He reached the sea-wall, braced himself against it and began to sprint towards them.

'Thank God we don't have children. They'd be psychopaths,' murmured Susan to Graham, who was now wicket keeper.

Before he could reply, Jeff had reached the pebble and bowled a full-pitch which knocked the bat out of his wife's hands and slapped against the bag. With a certain incredulity, Graham saw that Jeff was half-way down the makeshift pitch, his erect finger pointed at Susan in the obscene gesture of dismissal favoured by some Australian fast bowlers.

'Get back in ya bloody hutch!' roared Jeff in an accent noticeably removed from his quotidian stockbroker one. Susan widened her eyes at Graham, as one adult might to another about a child.

The next person in was Eliza who, again using the rounders stance, accumulated twelve runs, perhaps because Jeff seemed to bowl at her with rather less fire than at his wife and because Graham was even more diplomatic in his deliveries than he had been towards Susan. However, to the third delivery of Susan's first over – she was bowling underarm lobs – Eliza swung and spooned an easy catch to Jeff, who fumbled it but retrieved the ball before it hit the sand, his uncertainty perhaps the result of a struggle between natural competitiveness and other, newer emotions.

This brought Graham to the canvas bag. He chose an approach somewhere between rounders and authentic cricket, shoulders hunched but bat held horizontal so that he resembled a letter 'f' on an illuminated manuscript. Nervous of embarrassment by Jeff in front of Eliza, he was pleased that Susan was the first bowler he faced. Gripping the bat fiercely, he hit the first four of the match to the rock pool boundary. He had scored eight when Eliza came on for her first spell.

'I'm going to try over-arm, okay?' she shouted, and bounded in with steps like hopscotch before hurling the ball, with an arm transparently crooked, at her husband, missing both him and the hand luggage.

'Er, darling . . .' began Graham. The word came out 'dulling', that familiar marital parody carved by thoughtless repetition.

'Chucking!' protested Jeff. 'Bloody chucking!'

'I did what you and Graham did,' insisted Eliza. Jeff, shaking his head theatrically, ran towards her.

'No,' he explained. 'You've got to keep your arm straight. Otherwise it's what we call a no-ball.'

To reinforce what he was saying, he put an arm around Eliza's shoulders. 'A straight arm . . . (he stroked it) . . . from the shoulder . . . (he kneaded it) . . . the trick is, to keep your back very tight . . . (as illustration, he rubbed both hands very firmly across and around Eliza's spine) . . . you can only do that by getting side-on . . . (he turned her, holding her against the template of his own body) . . . and putting this leg down first . . . (he distinguished between the two relevant limbs by slapping the one he meant and making an emphatic gesture with his hand along its length) . . . do you want to try it?'

To Graham's delight, this torrent of advice from Jeff so confused Eliza that her next few deliveries were slow floaters which allowed him to advance his score to seventeen. Now he faced Jeff's bowling for the first time. The first two deliveries were so quick that he missed them in a hiss of sand, the third banged his knee – 'LBW!' shouted Jeff, 'bloody LBW!' – and the fourth, which he also missed, would have threatened any glassware Eliza might have stowed in the canvas bag.

'G.P. Sterling bowled Donald, 17,' Jeff blurted, grabbing the bat.

Perhaps predictably, he insisted, despite his height and the dwarf implement, on a classic stance, with the bat held vertically and tapping the sand. Thus hunched, he looked like a man who had got his tie caught in a trap-door while climbing out. Jeff proved, as Graham had feared, to be a natural stroke-maker, and was undefeated on 37, only partially flattered by the tide-diminished leg-side boundary and a dropped catch by Eliza, when sea stopped play.

The activity had made them hungry and they were at their sea-view table in Cliff's restaurant by seven o'clock. The radio reported that play had ended for the day in the Test match with the West Indies past 650 for the loss of four wickets.

There was a long wait for their sea-food starters and Graham was coveting the bread-basket. Eliza slapped his hand as he contemplated another bap. 'Darling, we don't want you any larger.'

Even though she had avoided saying 'fatter', he was troubled by any public discussion of his bulk. Eliza said to Jeff: 'Just like a Las Vegas gambler, my husband. Always one last roll . . .'

It was during the salmon en croûte that Jeff made his suggestion. 'Look, I suspect that even Lizzy, though she would never admit it, found this afternoon quite fun. Why don't we see if we can buy a proper wooden bat and stumps – not full-size but bigger kids' kind of thing – and have a game tomorrow afternoon? I mean, unless the girls are planning some sun-worship . . .'

Eliza, with a shiver, mentioned an article she had read about skin cancer rates in Miami.

'Okay, Jeff, for you, I will,' she conceded with an air which passed among friends as pretend-coquette.

Jeff wondered if, this time, they might not have teams. Susan said that would be fine but boys against girls would be unfair. Jeff proposed himself and Lizzy against Gray and you, darling. Dulling.

'Wife-swapping!' gasped Eliza. 'Listen, that's a thought. Does that kind of thing still go on? Or did it all die out in the sixties with Bob and Carol and Ted and Alice?'

'I think it's much more now, as it were, one-on-one adultery,' Susan replied.

Eliza remembered having read an article about AIDS reducing the incidence of adultery. Susan wondered if perhaps the virus had only reduced the admission of infidelity. Jeff felt that surely if people wanted to do that kind of thing, and he had colleagues who were still at it like dogs after truffles, AIDS or no AIDS, then surely they were just careful. Rubber and so on. Susan looked sharply out to sea as if she had seen a ship in distress there.

Across the profiteroles the conversation turned to books and then, because Jeff was being left out, to books about cricket.

'A really surprising number of quite famous writers have liked cricket,' Graham began, his speech more fluent than usual, for this was a subject on which he was certain of his expertise.

'In a minute he'll mention that Samuel Beckett is in *Wisden*,' interrupted Eliza.

'Darling . . .'

'Sorry . . .'

'Give him a chance, Lizzy . . .'

'I was just thinking,' continued Graham. 'Do you know, there's actually a team of English playwrights, having matches in the summer? Harold Pinter's the captain, so the club tie has three dots on it . . . that's a, er, pause . . . And he slips cricket into his plays. There's a line in one of them, "Who watered the wicket at Melbourne?" . . .'

'But the German translator,' Eliza jumped in again, 'not being as interested in cricket as all English people are and knowing only the military application of "wicket", construed the line as "Who urinated on the city gate at Melbourne?" . . .'

'Darling . . .'

'Eliza, stop this. We're enjoying Graham's story even if you're not . . .'

For Graham, Susan's intervention had the feel of getting your mother to come and sort out a rougher boy at school, and the next anecdote, which he had resolved to be the last, held the embarrassment of realising that the room or house in which you have been singing to yourself is not empty.

'And, in "The Go-Between", which Pinter adapted, there's that scene in which the messenger catches out Alan Bates in the cricket match as, of course, he'll catch them out later on . . .'

The evening ended, over port and brandy, in Cliff's Sea View Lounge, staring out at the darkness where water and sand were indistinguishable, the sea announced only by its noises; a radio play now where, that afternoon, it had been a technicolor movie. Jeff and Graham discussed the prospects of a young player making his England debut, from whom much would be required the following day (that year they were experimenting with Test match play on Sundays).

'He's got buckets of runs for his county,' Graham argued.

'Yeah? And how is he out, virtually always? Slips

or keeper. You've got to know where your off-stump is, got to. If you don't know where your off-stump is you're always going to be caught . . .'

'That sounds like good advice,' said Susan. She seemed to be looking at Graham.

In bed that night Graham, tentative as ever in this respect, tried an exploratory tickle between Eliza's legs but she diverted his attention with what she would not have known to call a forward defensive stroke.

'I'm too sleepy. You boys, you've tired me out with all that cricket.'

Sunday was the day of the collapse. West Indies had declared overnight and the first two English wickets were down by the time the four weekenders, who had risen late, finished with the Sunday papers over Cliff's Brunch. It was nearly one o'clock.

'I, er, think I might wander into town and look for the cricket stuff,' said Graham. 'Coming?'

That was to Jeff, who replied: 'I think I'm quite nicely settled in here, if that's okay, Gray.'

'No, that's fine. Darling?'

'I think I'd better digest Cliff's Brunch if I'm to be any use at all to Jeff this afternoon.'

'Okay. I'll be about an hour.'

Graham set off up the incline. If Jeff habitually conducted himself like someone who thought he was in a Hollywood movie, then Graham's demeanour was that of someone who feared they were being recorded by a store surveillance camera. As he strolled off he was a man self-consciously attempting to look normal.

A couple of minutes later Susan stood up, shaking a fat fan of discarded sections from one of the Sunday newspapers off her knees. 'I think I'd prefer to walk off my brunch. I'm going up there.' She gestured vaguely at one of the cliffs in the distance. 'I'll be back at two o'clock.'

'Okay, Sue.'

'Cheers, darling.' Dulling.

In the next hour, three incidents were witnessed by three different casual observers, all of whom drew the wrong conclusion from them.

Graham found and purchased a Beach Cricket Set which included a passably stout bat, four stumps, a set of bails and a tennis ball. As he paid, the shop-keeper – who might have been a sister of Mrs Owner – said 'For the kids?' Graham nodded.

Susan followed a gravelled footpath up past the hotel, treading hard, as if she was trying to wipe something unpleasant from her shoes. She found a bench on a peak and sat there, sometimes consulting her watch, as if she was awaiting an appointment. She threw stones in high arcs before their sudden plummet into the sea, hundreds of feet below.

A holidaying couple walked past in gaudy checked leisure wear from the Men's and Women's departments of the same prestige convenience store. They were playing a game, one of many innocuous diversions that had sustained their marriage. The trick was to construct a rapid biography for a stranger. They selected Susan for this exercise and put in their bids as they passed.

'Widow,' said the woman. 'First holiday alone, remembering.'

'Spinster,' said the man. 'Look at the way she's giving it to those stones. Sexual frustration.'

The woman playfully hit him, for what was clearly a stock response.

And, five minutes after Graham and Susan had disappeared from sight in opposite directions, Eliza and Jeff rose, leaving a mess of the Sunday press on the hotel terrace, and went inside.

Two pensioners, whose breakfast had been a pantomime of measuring out each other's medication, had been at the adjoining table since before the arrival of the four youngest guests, but had misread the alliances. Now they showed their eroded teeth to each other.

'Bet I know where they're going,' said the husband. 'Newly-weds, I bet.'

Afterwards, in the sea-view bedroom which the Sterlings had booked, Jeff, to Eliza's disquiet, flicked on the bedside radio and, with some difficulty, tuned it to Radio 3 to discover that England had lost another wicket. The débutant batsman had been caught behind driving, without, said the commentator, knowing where his off-stump was.

'Told him!' hissed Jeff. 'Bloody told him!'

Jeff and Eliza versus Graham and Susan began at 2.30 p.m. on a pitch similar to that of the previous afternoon.

The boundaries were unchanged, although the rules had been altered. Both players of the batting side would be at the wicket simultaneously, with their opponents sharing the bowling. To guarantee a match of reasonable length, each couple would bat for ten overs, with their total score divided by the number of dismissals. Jeff and Eliza won the toss and elected to bat.

The most notable feature of this innings was that Susan was a different bowler from the day before. She seemed somehow newly motivated, still propelling the ball underarm, but on the crouch, so that the proximity of her hand to the sand produced such a low trajectory that delivery after delivery – particularly when Eliza was at the wicket – could only be forced back towards her. Even Jeff's strokeplay was inhibited by this trick. After vainly attempting to drive four successive balls from his wife, Jeff shouted 'Cheating! Cheating!'

'You accuse *me* of cheating?' asked Susan. 'I'm sorry, I'll read that again. You accuse me of *cheating*?'

'It's not strictly against the rules,' Graham interceded. 'It's called a grub ball.'

'A grub ball,' said Susan, using the adjective like mouthwash. 'How very interesting.'

When it was Graham's turn to bowl, he again treated Eliza gently. Susan, retrieving the ball from the rock-pool boundary, walked up and handed it to Graham.

'You're making it easy for her.'

'Well, she's – this will sound silly – but she's my wife.'

'Oh, God. You don't know, do you?'

'Know what?'

'I ignore it but you actually don't realise. I wonder which of us is more dumb.'

'I'm sorry, I . . .'

'Oh, never mind.'

But the brief team talk did seem to have had some effect, as Graham clean bowled his wife twice in his last three overs. In her penultimate spell, one of Susan's grub balls squirmed off Jeff's bat as he swung at it and dislodged the bails. Susan stalked down the pitch, her finger up like a parody phallus, and whispered, in a manner deliberately measured, 'Get back in your hutch!'

At the end of their ten overs Jeff and Eliza had scored 44 for five dismissals. It was this average of just below nine which Graham and Susan would need to beat. As Graham counselled his partner before they started, 10 for once out would do, or 20 for twice; defence was probably, on balance, the better idea. And then, himself surprised by the words as they emerged, 'I'll take Jeff, as far as I can. I'll leave Eliza to you.'

Jeff, returning to the sea wall before each ball, bowled with speed and, to Graham's mind, frequently wide enough for an umpire to have intervened if there had been one. But, with solid defence and some frantic scampering between the wickets – there seemed to be an understanding between the batspersons – Graham and Susan reached 13 without any dismissals by the end of the eighth over. The ninth was Eliza's last, with Susan taking strike. She took two off the second ball and two off the fourth, both slightly lucky swipes towards the oncoming tide; but on the sixth delivery she flailed inelegantly and the ball ballooned off bat and bikini bottom high towards the sea, where Jeff, running round, caught it, probably with more fuss than was necessary. It was now 17 for once out and, as Jeff screeched to the nearly empty beach, 'all three results are still possible!'

On the first ball of the final over, Jeff seemed to be running with even more urgency than before. As Graham waited, there was a BBC cricket commentator in his head.

'And Sterling, who's scored 11 of the 17 runs, taps his bat in the crease as Donald, seagulls circling overhead, hurtles in and bowls, and that lifts and hits him and . . . I think that's hurt him.'

It had, having landed in the most vulnerable part of his trunks. Graham doubled up, his sight a rainstorm at sunset and his testicles as tender as peeled prawns. Pulling back towards comprehension, he noticed that Jeff was involved in an operatic rendition of 'Gotcha! Gotcha!' and reflected that this seemed unusually juvenile even for him, until the restored circumference of almost normal sight permitted him to see that the bails had been dislodged.

'Poor sod, you've played on off your balls,' boomed Jeff. 'It's 17 for twice out, which means we've won unless you get another two runs.'

As Jeff commenced his long march back, Susan arrived at Graham's side.

'Okay?'

'You, er, forget how much it hurts . . . not since school . . .'

'I want to win this, Graham, and I don't want any of that bollocks – sorry! – about it only being a game. I've never even beaten him at Monopoly. So, come on.'

As Graham took guard again, the game had become a grudge match: Susan's was, quite specifically, against Jeff and Eliza, while Graham's, more unfocussed, something he could never have verbally expressed, was against all those thinner, richer, surer males who had bettered him since the Under-Nine County Trials. It was a line to which Jeff Donald was merely the latest pretender.

As he waited, the commentator was in his head again.

'And Sterling, a brave little fighter, won't let that knock worry him. Donald in, and that's a good, straight ball and Sterling plays it very correctly back. No run. Still 17 for two and, Trevor, we've had a cake . . .'

The third and fourth balls were too wide for Graham to reach. Susan made a 'come on' face from the other end. Jeff set off to bowl the penultimate ball of the match.

'. . . and Donald, in the late afternoon light, really rather a beautiful sight this Cliff's ground, races in, bowls and Sterling swings and, oh dear, I think he's in the wars again . . .'

He was. Missing the ball, which luckily also missed the stumps, he had diverted a thick squirt of sand into his face and, specifically, his eyes. Ruinous instinct led him to dash towards the sea where he scooped salt water into his dry, tight, fiery sockets. The brine did not help and it was only when the more practical Susan arrived at his side with a towel and bottled drinking water that passable repairs were effected.

'You can retire hurt if you want,' offered Jeff.

'I don't think so,' replied Graham, and walked back to the pitch. If he squinted, the pain was scarcely more than a small irritation. He peered around. He must hit the ball towards the sea, an area covered only by Eliza running round from behind the stumps. Jeff was ready.

'Last ball of the match. One run will tie the match, two will give it to Graham Sterling's team. And what a captain's innings it has been. And here's Donald . . . thundering in . . . bowls and it's down the leg side and Sterling swings and he's mis-hit it and it's going high in the air, very high, and they've run one and they're coming back and both Jeff Donald and Eliza Sterling are racing over the sand towards the ball. They look like, well, like lovers running across a beach. And the ball is still in the air, and Eliza Sterling dives and she's caught it – she's caught it! – caught her own husband – and she's given victory to her side!'

And through a mist of grit and brine, Graham, throwing down the bat, saw Jeff and Eliza, flat on the sand, roll over, kneel and celebrate their victory with a hug.

Retired Hurt

DONALD TRELFORD

I WAS FIFTEEN and it was my first innings for the school First XI. As I walked nervously out to open the batting on the lush, sedate playing fields of Warwick School, I was relieved to see a black Ford Escort pulling up by the rope at the third man boundary.

It meant that my parents had managed to drive there in time from Coventry (we were playing away), even though my father had been working on the Saturday morning. My selection was a bit of a surprise for all of us, as I had been drafted in at short notice after scoring a mid-week fifty in a house match. I raised my bat towards the car in acknowledgement.

A few balls later I was looking towards them again – cheerily at first, as I could see that my cut would beat third man, then with mounting horror, as the ball raced towards the gleaming car, jumped as it hit the boundary rope, and struck the front bumper with a sickening crack that echoed round the ground.

My natural pleasure at breaking my duck was banished by the thought of that awful dent on the new car. I knew that my first scoring stroke in serious cricket would be talked about for a long time to come, and not for reasons to do with cricket.

My fears were realised at the end of the over when my father emerged from the car, took a cloth and some polish, bent down with his back to the play and proceeded to work on the dent for the rest of my innings. He didn't watch another ball. There was no unkindness in the gesture – he was proud of the 25 I scored that day: it simply showed a grown-up's sense of priorities.

My father had introduced me to the game nearly ten years before when he had come home on leave from the army with a cricket bat.

It was a heavy great thing that still stands, repaired now at the splice with a patch of metal, in the corner of his garden shed. It is still almost too heavy for me to hold comfortably now, never mind as a toddler.

We had been evacuated to a village in County Durham, where cricket bats, especially in war-time, were few and far between. Suddenly I found myself the most sought-after person in the village, as older boys called round at the house and suggested a game. I had no idea how to play, but happily trailed after them, basking in my new-found popularity.

As the owner of the bat I was accorded the honour of the first knock. At this point my total ignorance of the game became apparent. After some initial uncertainty as to which way round to hold it and whether I was left- or right-handed, I was given my first lesson in how to grip a cricket bat. I recommend it to any young starter today. I was told: 'lay the bat on the ground with the handle towards you and pick it up as if you were about to club someone on the head with it, like a caveman. Then bring it down into position by your legs without changing the grip.' I've never played any other way. Not that it did me much good on that first occasion, for I found that I could scarcely lift the bat, and was quickly bowled out for the first of many ducks.

Property rights having been perfunctorily acknowledged in this way, and the basic courtesies observed, I was thereafter dismissed to sit on the fence overlooking the railway line while my bat was put to more productive use by the other boys. The fence was one of my favourite places. The whole village had rushed there one night as the royal train passed through, and we often came to jeer at the Italian prisoners-of-war labouring on the tracks. They used to grin back, some of them, and invite us to share their hunk of bread.

After the war my family had returned to Coventry, which made me an ex-officio fan of Warwickshire cricket. Twice a year the county side came to the city to play at the grim Courtaulds ground, fenced in by corrugated iron and swept by the fumes of the chemical factory.

I had a privileged place there because my best friend's

father was captain of the Courtaulds club. We were allowed to practise on the patch of ground behind the scoreboard while opening batsman Fred Gardner, his face like an unsmiling Bob Hope, accumulated runs with the speed of drying paint.

In the school holidays we took the train to Birmingham and then a 48 bus to Edgbaston. 'Took the train' was a euphemism for scrambling aboard without a ticket as the train slowed at the corner outside Foleshill station, dragging our Dad's Army haversacks, laden with pop, crisps and spam, through the window behind us. I still have a flattened thumbnail from banging the carriage door too quickly on one of these stowaway excursions.

I have three memories of Bradman's Australians, the big draw of 1948. One is my first sight of the great Don himself, going out for the toss in a three-piece suit and a trilby hat. Another is of Keith Miller rolling out to the wicket swinging his bat, heaving mightily and missing his first ball, hitting a six off the second, holing out in the deep off the third, and swinging his bat nonchalantly all the way back to the pavilion. His side, I might add, had 400 on the board at that time.

The most powerful memory, though is of seeing Eric Hollies bowl Bradman with a googly – a trick he repeated ten days later in Bradman's last Test, deceiving him second ball and leaving him poised for eternity on that tantalising average of 99.9.

My Warwickshire heroes were Tom Pritchard, a New Zealand quickie who took 166 wickets at an average of 15 in 1948; Tom Dollery, the captain, whose bat seemed as broad as the proverbial barn door; A.H. Kardar, an elegant left-hander who went on to play for both India and Pakistan; Alan Townsend, the nippiest slip fielder I ever saw; Bert Wolton, an elegant upright hitter with immaculate Brylcreemed black hair; and Dick Spooner, a stumper in the old sense who actually stumped batsmen out, usually off Eric Hollies.

I was present when Test cricket returned to Edgbaston in 1957, for what turned out to be, in the words of *Wisden*, 'one of the most remarkable matches of all time.' After Ramadhin had bowled England out on the first day, the West Indies took a massive first innings lead, with 161 from Colley Smith, a powerful striker who later died in a car crash. The sun was so fierce on the Saturday that I went home with one side of my face burned and the other not. On the Monday and into Tuesday England were saved by the historic partnership of 411 between Peter May and Colin Cowdrey, and finally came close to winning the match.

Nearly 30 years later, at the Kensington Oval in Bridgetown, Barbados, I saw the West Indies humble England in return. My ticket had been delivered to me at my hotel by Sir Garfield Sobers himself. During the game my colleagues in the press box were amused when a messenger came to announce: 'Mr Trelford, the Prime Minister would like to see you.' 'Which Prime Minister?' I said. (As it happened, I had also got to know another Caribbean Prime Minister, Michael Manley of Jamaica, when I chaired a lively meeting at the Riverside Studios in Hammersmith to launch his history of West Indian cricket.)

What lingers most vividly about Barbados, however, is not the speed of the West Indies attack, nor the craven submission of the England batsmen, nor even a lively dinner with Mr and Mrs Phil Edmonds, but the legendary après-cricket consumption of Ian Botham on a boat, the *Bajan Queen*, on that famous night he met Miss Barbados . . .

These nostalgic thoughts have been provoked by the sight of my present bat – undoubtedly my last – standing in the corner of my study. Having ripped a calf muscle in the field in my last game and hobbled around on crutches for several months since, I am naturally inclined to wonder if I shall ever hold it again. When I last took it to be repaired, the man asked me how old I was. When I said 'Fifty', he replied. 'Bit of an optimist, aren't you, having a bat mended at your age?'

If that last match was the end, it was a most inglorious way to go. I had turned out for the *Observer* for the annual match against the *Sunday Times* at Teddington's lovely tree-lined ground in Bushey Park. We had only just started to play and it was already raining. Because it was so wet underfoot I had decided to wear my old school cricket boots with extra-long spikes. I lunged forward for a catch at mid-on but only got my fingertips to it. One ball later our wicket keeper, John Parker, whose son Paul, the Sussex batsman, has played for England, threw the ball back to me. It fell short and I moved forward to catch it. My spiky boots, however, stayed in the ground for a fraction longer, and the leg must have snapped with the strain. Exit crippled editor, pursued shortly afterwards by everyone else as the rain put paid to the match.

If that day has also finally put paid to my cricket career, then so be it. I have some happy memories to look back on, starting at school, where I went on to be captain of cricket. Two close reflex catches – one high at slip and the other at forward short-leg off a beamer – are as vivid today as the bruises they brought to my palm were then. In the RAF, where I spent more time on the cricket field than in the air, I remember a tour of Germany for which such words as riotous and rumbustious would be pallid euphemisms.

The high points at Cambridge, apart from the sheer delight of walking out to bat at Fenner's, were three sixes off successive balls at Selwyn and a 65 on a golden day on Jesus Green,. There was also a lively tour of Ireland during which I was stopped in Dublin as an IRA suspect while walking home from a dance in the early hours. To the eye of an Irish policeman, unfamiliar with cricket, my bag looked as if it might well contain a rifle. In later life I shall recall a 74 (out of 109) in my first match for the *Observer* against the *Sunday Times*, and five for twelve (and man of the match) bowling tweakers at Chelmsford.

My strongest memories of cricket, though, will not be of any personal triumphs, of which there were all too few, but of some curious incidents. One was of batting against the doctors at a mental hospital in Warwickshire while the patients clapped wildly at all the wrong moments, and of fielding on the boundary while they lobbed bricks perilously close to my head.

I shall never forget playing several seasons with the Adastrians, a club for past and present RAF officers. On one occasion my train from the north was very late, with the result that I dashed from Kings Cross in a taxi and arrived at Westminster Square in time to be told that we were batting, I was opening and the other side were already in the field. I changed in a blur and was caught behind off the second ball without stopping for breath. I looked up at the clock as I walked back to the pavilion and saw it was 11.32. The game would go on until 6.30, I reflected, and my part in it was already over.

I was determined to score a fifty at Vine Lane, the Adastrians' HQ. One year I made a 44 and then a 46. The next time, when I was 49 not out, I felt sure that I would make it. But I hadn't allowed for a stubborn Flight Lieutenant at the other end, who refused to exert himself for anyone else's runs. Several times I cut the ball to short wide third man and went for the vital run but he always sent me back. Finally, in exasperation, I played it to the fielder's left hand and charged down the pitch for what I judged to be an easy run. When I got to the other end I found my partner leaning on his bat and flatly refusing to budge. I turned back and was run out by a mile.

Not surprisingly, and to put it mildly, I was rather upset by this. When I reached the dressing room I saw that it seemed to be empty, whereupon I hurled my bat across it with a string of violent oaths. What I hadn't seen was a huge Air Marshal, one of the luminaries of RAF cricket, emerging from the washroom at the back.

He watched my antics with scarcely concealed mirth, then uttered from beneath his startling eyebrows some words of wisdom which I shall never forget and that I recall whenever I feel the need to keep a sense of proportion about life's little frustrations. 'Never mind,' he said. 'You'll get over it. Japs tried to cut my balls off in the war. I got over that.'

Let Them Eat Cake

EDWIN BROCK

We're spending the summer on Radio Three
From ten fifty-five until stumps are drawn
It's the TMS soap with non-stop commentary
From Bill Frindall, Trevor Bailey,
Henry Blofeld, Fred Trueman,
Old Uncle Brian Johnston and all,
Old Uncle Brian Johnston and all.

It takes place in a box with cream cakes on the floor
From ten fifty-five until stumps are drawn
And the W.I. ladies are baking lots more
For Bill Frindall, Trevor Bailey,
Henry Blofeld, Fred Trueman
Old Uncle Brian Johnston and all,
Old Uncle Brian Johnston and all.

Now one of the cast must be sporting a beard
From ten fifty-five until stumps are drawn
Which one of the others finds wondrously weird

With Bill Frindall, Trevor Bailey,
Henry Blofeld, Fred Trueman,
Old Uncle Brian Johnston and all,
Old Uncle Brian Johnston and all.

So they set him conundrums again and again
From ten fifty-five until stumps are drawn
To fill in the time between showers of rain
For Bill Frindall, Trevor Bailey,
Henry Blofeld, Fred Trueman,
Old Uncle Brian Johnston and all,
Old Uncle Brian Johnston and all.

And then they discuss every inch of the pitch
From ten fifty-five until stumps are drawn
The warp and the weft and the slope and the ridge
With Bill Frindall, Trevor Bailey,
Henry Blofeld, Fred Trueman,
Old Uncle Brian Johnston and all,
Old Uncle Brian Johnston and all.

The one they call Boil is dismissing the team
From ten fifty-five until stumps are drawn
And blunt Freddie Trueman blows off Yorkshire steam
To Bill Frindall, Trevor Bailey,
Henry Blofeld, Fred Trueman,
Old Uncle Brian Johnston and all,
Old Uncle Brian Johnston and all.

The posh one called Blowers is making a fuss
From ten fifty-five until stumps are drawn
At the sight of an ordinary red omnibus

To Bill Frindall, Trevor Bailey,
Henry Blofeld, Fred Trueman,
Old Uncle Brian Johnston and all,
Old Uncle Brian Johnston and all.

After half an hour's play the computers are out
From ten fifty-five until stumps are drawn
For an over-rate, run-rate, no-ball knockabout
From Bill Frindall, Trevor Bailey,
Henry Blofeld, Fred Trueman,
Old Uncle Brian Johnston and all,
Old Uncle Brian Johnston and all.

And then an assessment of who's going to win
From ten fifty-five until stumps are drawn
Based on the clouds and the strength of the wind
From Bill Frindall, Trevor Bailey,
Henry Blofeld, Fred Trueman,
Old Uncle Brian Johnston and all,
Old Uncle Brian Johnston and all.

And one of them must have a doctor's degree
From ten fifty-five until stumps are drawn
For diagnosis of fingers and backs and a knee
To Bill Frindall, Trevor Bailey,
Henry Blofeld, Fred Trueman,
Old Uncle Brian Johnston and all,
Old Uncle Brian Johnston and all.

They meet their old mates as they walk round the
 ground
From ten fifty-five until stumps are drawn

And come back in the box saying 'Guess who I
found . . .'
To Bill Frindall, Trevor Bailey,
Henry Blofeld, Fred Trueman,
Old Uncle Brian Johnston and all,
Old Uncle Brian Johnston and all.

For we used to have batsmen and bowlers as well
From ten fifty-five until stumps are drawn
But now they're old men with tall stories to tell
To Bill Frindall, Trevor Bailey,
Henry Blofeld, Fred Trueman,
Old Uncle Brian Johnston and all,
Old Uncle Brian Johnston and all.

Every now and again they remember the game
From ten fifty-five until stumps are drawn
But whenever they do things are always the same
For Bill Frindall, Trevor Bailey,
Henry Blofeld, Fred Trueman,
Old Uncle Brian Johnston and all,
Old Uncle Brian Johnston and all.

We're deep in the mire with our backs to the wall
From ten fifty-five until stumps are drawn
It's bad form, it's bad luck, it's the shape of the
ball
Say Bill Frindall, Trevor Bailey,
Henry Blofeld, Fred Trueman,
Old Uncle Brian Johnston and all,
Old Uncle Brian Johnston and all.

But we're saved by the bell for more cakes have arrived
From ten fifty-five until stumps are drawn
They'll keep up our peckers and help us survive
Bill Frindall, Trevor Bailey,
Henry Blofeld, Fred Trueman,
Old Uncle Brian Johnston and all,
Old Uncle Brian Johnston and all.

And each one that's eaten's acknowledged on air
From ten fifty-five until stumps are drawn
Which is not entertaining but is after all fair
Say Bill Frindall, Trevor Bailey,
Henry Blofeld, Fred Trueman,
Old Uncle Brian Johnston and all,
Old Uncle Brian Johnston and all.

For no-one talks cricket as well as they do
From ten fifty-five until stumps are drawn
They do it for England and they do it for you
They're Bill Frindall, Trevor Bailey,
Henry Blofeld, Fred Trueman,
Old Uncle Brian Johnston and all,
Old Uncle Brian Johnston and all.

So we're winning the prattle but losing the war
From ten fifty-five until stumps are drawn
And now Henry's bus has pulled up at the door
For Bill Frindall, Trevor Bailey,
Henry Blofeld, Fred Trueman,
Old Uncle Brian Johnston and all,
Old Uncle Brian Johnston and all.

The Southern Drifters

DAVID ENGLISH

I FIRST MET Norman Graham at his benefit game back in 1977. Brenchley in deepest Kent was the idyllic setting for the contest between the Vic Lewis All Stars and Norman Graham's Benefit XI. Bob Woolmer, like a young Colin Cowdrey, proceeded to delight all and sundry (or was it Saturday?) by clipping the ball off his toes into the hedgerows. Alan Ealham excelled in the covers and Clint punched the ball pugnaciously to all parts.

The sounds of summer were punctuated by the booming roar of 'Why aye man . . . yer drinking like a budgie!' This Geordie burr belonged to big Norman, who to my knowledge has always been six feet seven inches tall and thirty-nine years old. An amiable giant off the field, as a bowler Norm was a mean machine. Legs full of lager, he fired them in just short of a length, giving you a sound thud under the heart. This heady deckchair day was enjoyed by all. A few beakers afterwards in the beer tent, the vicar's two smashing daughters and a promise to meet Big Norm in a Mayfair Bierkeller the following day.

Mid-day in 'Munich' Norm and I swopped stories. We had both experienced a certain recent sadness and the lager helped inflame our mutual feeling for the cavalier and our desire to escape.

'Let's get together fourteen good lads, nutters with style, and go on tour.' Indeed, this seemed a sensible notion. By the time we spilled into Brook Street, The Southern Drifters had been born – destination Barbados. Little did we know that the Drifters would become a legendary force starring such luminaries as Browney, Sven Venables, Sir OG and Powerful Pierre.

CAPTAIN'S LOG – Barbados Tour

NOVEMBER – Gatwick – Shake 'n' Bake Airways to Barbados.

Accommodation – Flamboyant Avenue, Sunset Crest, Holetown.

Norm's Preparations for Big Game

Meet 7.30 p.m. in his villa (death row circled by vultures. I would happily have swopped Gary Gilmore's firing squad for one of Norm's 'quick' rum sessions). Then the motorcade of Mini Mokes threading their way along the Holed highway into Bridgetown, stopping off at every rum shack.

Dancing with the optics on the top shelf in 'The

Great Neck' club before attacking the night until every sinew in your body cried out for sleep. Then standing outside Aunty's watching the rising dawn, eating chicken while your head beat like an anvil in a hot dustbin. Big Norm, suitably satisfied that his troops were well and truly now in tip-top match condition, would then boom out the order to return home. There he would sit, giraffe-like in the leading Moke like Rommel, waving on the column of his demented tourists.

8.00 a.m. My head hit the pillow.

9.30 a.m. I was hurled to the floor by Norm with a rum punch in his hand. 'Come on man, drink up. We've got to be on the ground by eleven!'

The first game of the tour was against Barclays Bank. I opened the batting with a Geordie called Mickey Leishman. Mick had never been out of England. There he stood, brand new bat, pads, all the gear, taking in the wonders of this sun-drenched paradise.

In ran a stallion called Stamford, related to Sylvester Clarke (somehow they all are). His first ball felled Mickey like a stone, breaking his arm in three places. As the Geordie was despatched to Queen Elizabeth's Hospital, I was joined at the crease by R.M.O. 'Bobby' Cooke, a fellow left-hander. Squinting through tired eyes, he nicked one off his helmet for three.

In roared Stamford. Behind him a typical Caribbean backdrop. No sight screens, a couple of copulating goats and a blue, blue sky. The ball was up. Swish went the cover drive sending the red blur screaming over the slips for four.

When Cooke had scored a kamikaze thirty-two, all of which flew past third man's head, Stamford took it upon himself to issue the following warning of impending doom. 'I'll hit you on de head man.' Pretending not to have heard him I took a pace forward and with considerable dignity tapped down the wicket as befitted an Englishman abroad. In ran Stamford, his arms ramming like pistons. The ball was short. I was determined to smack it. The ground went quiet. Parakeets teetered atop the baying palms. All eyes were focused on my cranium as it recoiled from the impact of Stamford's delivery.

Down I went. A veil of crimson obliterated my mind. I had gone. As I came around I looked up and saw Big Norman holding out his hand and smiling all over his Walter Matthau phizzog. 'Why aye Dave, can you see my fingers?' I was carried off the field and taken down to the 'Bone Orchard'. Mickey Leishman was coming out of the hospital, his arm mummified, as I was told to sit in the casualty department.

Next to me, sprawled on his seat, was a man head thrown back, fast asleep. 'I've just been hit on the head by a bouncer,' I reported chirpily. 'Look: can you see here? It was Stamford Clarke.' Pointing to my wound, I tried to arouse some sympathy from my sleeping partner. Just then the door of the surgery opened. Out walked a doctor who looked at me blankly. 'No point talking to Leroy,' he said. 'He's dead!' Somehow, suddenly I felt much better. In walked a drunk, hopelessly out of sync, wearing a red shirt. Guiding him to my left, I continued my search for sympathy. 'Don't bother talking to Leroy, he's dead,' I blurted. 'Look: I've just been hit on the head by a bouncer . . . Stamford C . . .' As I spoke my new friend lolled back, his eyeballs set deep in their hollows. 'I've just been stabbed in the back . . .' he gurgled, before slumping on to the floor. Sure enough the shirt was red with blood, after a knifing incident involving an American sailor in the Bel Air Jazz Club.

Compared to my two companions, I now felt bloody marvellous. However, as I rose to leave, the doctor called me in and stitched me up. Cricketers have pop star status on the island and he wanted to know all the details including Stamford's exact bowling figures.

'Many thanks doc,' I said as I prepared to leave. 'What's the form, antibiotics and no alcohol?'

'No man,' replied the medic with a big smile. 'Plenty of rum and pokey pokey!' With that he returned to his surgery, from which came the strains of Bob Marley and the Wailers.

When I went back to the ground it resembled something like the battle of Flanders Field. Six more of the lads were walking wounded, heading for the hospital.

Barbados has never been the same. During the past ten years the Southern Drifters under the leadership of Kommandant Norm have continued to tour the world leaving a trail of devastation in their wake.

Graham Clinton, a Surrey man for the past decade, has continued to open the innings in his own gutsy style, never letting the side down. This season, just before he went out to bat at the Oval, I reported to him the stories about Big Norm. He smiled. He had heard them all before. Nothing had changed since Brenchley in 1977. And with that, Clint strode out, took on the new ball and as usual gave his team a cracking start.

As a fellow left-hander, I feel sure he would have hooked that bouncer in Barbados or left well alone!

Did George Orwell Get It Right?

JOHN TIMPSON

ALL RIGHT, SO George Orwell was never a big name on the sports pages, but occasionally he put aside his preoccupation with big brothers and bossy animals to observe the sporting scene, and he was not impressed by what he saw.

'Serious sport,' he decided, 'has nothing to do with fair play. It is bound up with hatred, jealousy, boastfulness, disregard for all rules, and sadistic pleasure in witnessing violence. In other words it is war minus the shooting.'

Now you might argue that he meant boxing, or all-in wrestling, or either kind of football, but surely not cricket, that most gentlemanly of pursuits? Ho-ho . . .

It starts at school, with the hatred and jealousy. I was a cricketer of such outstanding mediocrity that I was bitterly jealous of just about everybody, and those who were really good at it I hated quite violently.

Then for one intoxicating season, because I was older and taller than everyone else left in my group – my contemporaries had moved on to higher things – I was made captain of the Seventh Eleven. Orwell allowed for this situation too. Just as he forecast, I boasted about it incessantly.

There were not many schools that ran seven elevens, and our opponents were mostly the odds and ends who had to be found some sort of occupation on a Wednesday afternoon to keep them off the streets. But then, basically, so were we, and we were trounced week after week. As captain I bore the brunt of our games master's opprobrium: he seemed to worry about such things rather more than we did. But I did have the consolation of being able to select my own fielding position, and in my innocence I appointed myself wicket keeper.

It seemed a good idea at the time. I was renowned for my incompetence as a bowler or fielder, and I was used to spending my time in the field banished to some distant corner of the boundary, where it was everybody's devout hope, including mine, that I would never have to encounter the ball. As captain, however, I was expected to take a more central part in the proceedings, within reasonable range of the goings-on at the wicket. I was well aware that if a ball was struck towards me at short range I would be incapable of either catching it or avoiding it, and that sooner or later I would suffer physical injury. If I lurked behind the wicket, I thought, not only would I have the protection of gloves and pads but I would not be expected to run very far in any direction.

I had not reckoned on the arrival of the Demon Bowler.

He joined us towards the end of the season. Until then he had been playing in one of the more senior elevens, but I gathered that the ferocity of his bowling was matched only by its inaccuracy, and although he was very good at terrorising batsmen he rarely achieved a dismissal, except by maiming them. For anyone seeking 'sadistic pleasure in witnessing violence' the Demon Bowler was there to provide it. Following several complaints from opposing teams he was eventually sent to our school equivalent of the penalty box, or sin-bin – the Seventh Eleven.

I am not quite sure how I managed to upset him. It may have been after the two wides with which he opened his first over, when I strolled down the pitch to administer a gentle captain's rebuke. He seemed to accept it with ill grace, if I judged his gesture and his muttered comment aright. Or it may have been the result of his third delivery, which was unexpectedly so straight that it took both the batsman and myself unawares. The batsman allowed it to clip the edge of the bat, and I allowed it to clip the edge of my gloves. It then disappeared towards the boundary.

The Demon, having leapt a foot or two in the air at the first touch, emitted a terrible cry at the second, as triumph gave place to disappointment. It sounded like 'Howzzhit!'

The pattern of his bowling then underwent a subtle change. He no longer attempted to hit the wicket, if that indeed had been his plan. Nor, for once, did he hit the batsman. I became increasingly certain that he was trying to hit me.

The full-tosses came through like cannon-balls, about a foot above the stumps. The batsman, no doubt appreciating what was happening, kept well out of the way. I managed to fend off a couple of them, then I kept out of the way too, only to be reprimanded by the umpire, whose sadistic pleasure would have done Orwell's heart good.

'Stand up to them, Timpson!' he cried.

No coconut ever felt more vulnerable.

In those days we played eight balls to an over, and thanks to the two wides the Demon had seven deliveries after that dropped catch to take his revenge. The bombardment seemed to go on for ever, but somehow I survived, with nothing worse than the odd bruise. But I was not going to risk another over. As captain I still held the trump card; I took the wretched fellow off. We lost the game, of course, but at least I could still walk.

By now you may be nodding sagely. 'Ah, yes,' you will be saying, 'such behaviour may occur among irresponsible schoolboys, but when players mature they grow out of this childish behaviour. It could not happen in club or county cricket.'

I'm sorry, but ho-ho again . . .

There was this Minor Counties side which needed to

win the final match of the season to become champions of their Division. A draw would not be enough. They batted first and set up a useful total. Their opponents never looked like catching up, but the wickets were slow to fall. The last two batsmen were still there and looking reasonably comfortable at the start of the final over, but they needed 24 runs to win, an apparently impossible target. Everyone assumed they would settle for a draw, and play out the over with the utmost caution.

If the Demon Bowler had been playing that day I am fairly sure what his tactics would have been. Orwell talked of 'war minus the shooting' but to the batsmen it would have felt just like the real thing. The bowler in this case, however, did not have the speed for such a lethal attack, even if he had the inclination. He was able to bowl with considerable accuracy but at a fairly gentle pace. A straight bat, held firmly in front of the stumps, was about all the defence one required. A draw seemed inevitable.

I do not know whether it was he or his captain who devised the Machiavellian scheme which overcame this impasse. I do know that, while it did not quite amount to Orwell's 'disregard for all rules', as an exercise in gamesmanship it made John McEnroe look like an amateur . . .

As the bowler started his over he seemed to take particular care with his run-up. It soon became apparent why. He was anxious that when the ball left his hand his feet would *not* be in the correct position relative to the crease. Quite deliberately he sent down a gentle no-ball, then another, then another . . .

The batsmen could hardly believe their good fortune. They let fly. By the time the sixth no-ball had been delivered they had knocked up fourteen gift-wrapped runs, and with at least six more balls to come they seemed to be in sight of a possible victory. Understandably, they threw caution to the winds.

It was precisely what that devious bowler had planned. After the sixth no-ball he corrected his run and started bowling accurately. Instead of blocking the balls as they would have done ten minutes earlier, the batsmen made a desperate attempt to knock up the remaining runs. The last wicket duly fell, and the victors gained the necessary points to overtake the leaders and win the title.

It so happened that the leaders, who had been watching this helplessly from afar, were my own county of Norfolk, which is why I find myself somewhat in sympathy with Mr Orwell. All is fair, it seems, in love, war and Minor Counties cricket. But my faith in the game was restored when Norfolk decided not to contest the result, even though it robbed them of their first chance to win the divisional championship since 1913. Their chairman called it 'pure farce bordering on cheating,' and left it at that. I am glad he did not add, 'It's not cricket!' because I am sure we would have heard from George Orwell a sepulchral ho-ho . . .

Bowled Over

BRIAN WALDEN

IF DOUGLAS JARDINE is gazing down on the contemporary cricket scene from the great leg-trap in the sky, he must be consumed by a deep inner satisfaction. His theories of how international cricket should be played have been copied by every country which has the players capable of turning cricket into a battle of fear and intimidation.

What would make a particular appeal to Jardine's sense of irony is that cricket's governing bodies have done nothing to prevent this intimidation and do not wish the subject to be discussed. They have no intention of changing the laws of the game, or even of having the existing laws effectively enforced. The cricketing establishment won its battle with Jardine, but it lost the war. It will not admit this, because to do so would raise fundamental questions not only about the regulation of the game, but about its very nature.

The essence of cricket's enchantment lies in its

subtlety. Who does not thrill to watch the skill of Pakistan's great leg-spinner Abdul Qadir, or to read of the beautifully deceptive flight of legendary left-arm slow bowlers like Wilfred Rhodes and Colin Blythe? That is the cricket we want to see and hear stories about. But have we, aided by cricket's greatest writers, Cardus, Moyes, Robinson, James and Swanton, been deceiving ourselves? Could not a case be made that in cricket the best results are secured not by subtlety, but by brute force?

Fast bowlers, when used properly, have always been a decisive influence in first-class cricket. One need only think of the great Surrey team of the 1890s built around Richardson and Lockwood. We are told that Tom Richardson never pitched short intentionally, and was upset if he struck an opposing batsman. But the same is not true of his Australian contemporary Ernest Jones, who regularly bowled bouncers and took pleasure in his ability to intimidate batsmen. It is claimed that in one match at Nottingham those great openers Arthur Shrewsbury and William Gunn deliberately got themselves out rather than risk life and limb against Jones.

I have a suspicion that much went on in cricket before the First World War over which a veil has been drawn. We do know that Plum Warner in 1910 objected vigorously to the bowling of Burns of Worcestershire. At Lord's, Burns bowled something that sounds suspiciously like Jardine's 'bodyline'. But in those days the game was under aristocratic control and teams could be discouraged from experimenting with potentially successful techniques of intimidation by being told: 'this is not cricket'. A word to the wise was all that was needed.

Warwick Armstrong, Australia's skipper immediately after the First World War, was not a man who took the slightest notice of aristocrats, legislators, or anybody else for that matter. He did as he pleased. He had two great fast bowlers, Jack Gregory and Ted Macdonald, and he used them ruthlessly. As far as I can judge, Armstrong was responsible for an innovation for which he has received insufficient credit. He bowled his fast bowlers in tandem at the start of an innings. Previously, the prevailing theory had favoured a sharp difference in pace at the two ends. It was Armstrong who grasped how intense could be the psychological pressure of unremitting speed at both ends.

That at least one of Armstrong's bowlers consistently relied upon intimidation is hardly in dispute. In my youth I chatted for hours with men, including my father, who had seen much of Gregory's bowling in 1921. They all told the same story. Gregory sent down a stream of bouncers and the ball regularly whizzed past the batsman's head. Batsmen were afraid of him. Let us cut through the sophistries that often appear in cricket books when that phrase is used. Batsmen were not afraid that they might be caught in the slips, or have their stumps uprooted. They were frightened of physical injury, and many of them took evasive action by backing away to square-leg.

Why was this not openly admitted at the time? This is perhaps the key question when considering intimidatory fast bowling. To concede that first-class batsmen have good reason to be afraid of being hurt by short-pitched fast bowling is to acknowledge that it is an effective bowling technique. But, if that is the case, then any side that wants to be successful should use as many intimidatory bowlers as it can find. That awful logic was more than Establishment opinion in the Twenties could face, and to this day it has difficulty in admitting that its beloved game can have its subtle balance completely upset by a crude and unsporting ploy.

So the reaction to Gregory's bowling was muddled. On the one hand it was described as 'fearsome'; on the other, a parade of old-timers was assembled to explain that he was bowling long-hops, which their generation would have hooked to the boundary, or over it. This began a fashion which has persisted to the present day. Eventually, there will be a fast bowler who stands seven feet ten inches in his socks and hurls down the short stuff at 120 m.p.h. We shall be told that if batsmen used the hook-shot properly, in the manner of MacLaren, McCabe and Compton, the bowling would present few problems. Only when somebody is killed will there be a universal admission that a problem exists which requires a change in the laws of the game.

Jardine did bring about a change in the laws. A cold realist, tutored by Percy Fender, who never got on well with the cricket establishment, Jardine not only encouraged Larwood, Voce and Bowes to pitch short, but set a massed leg-side field to capitalise on attempts by the batsman to use his bat to protect himself. That was the essence of 'bodyline' and it soon became a prohibited form of attack. But banning the leg-side field did not go to the root of the problem. Where that lay was best revealed by the remarkable skill of Harold Larwood. He was very fast, very accurate and very fit in 1932-33. It is always implied that he hit batsmen because the leg-side field discouraged them from making a stroke. That is true, but it is also true that he hit batsmen who were attempting to play a shot. It was right to ban the leg-side field, but wrong to suppose that without such a field short-pitched fast bowling lost its point.

The proof that bouncers could demoralise professional batsmen, even without a packed leg-side field, was most clearly demonstrated after the Second World War by Lindwall and Miller. Naturally those great bowlers, like Gregory and Larwood, had skills that went far beyond the ability to deliver the ball half-way down the pitch. That is not the point. Bouncers do not take many wickets, because that is not their purpose. What they do is to scare batsmen, so that balance and correct footwork are lost and the fast bowler's good-length deliveries reap a rich reward. It is of little use to say that batsmen ought not to be afraid and must fearlessly get into the line of flight without worrying whether the ball is rearing up at their heads or not.

If they had that mental attitude, they might be better suited to boxing than to cricket. Admittedly, the ball is hard and the game is not for cowards, but how much physical risk is a batsman expected to take?

Any illusions about what fast bowlers were doing, and why they were doing it, ought to have been removed by watching Dennis Lillee and Jeff Thomson. Not only did they hit batsmen and look as if they were trying to hit batsmen, they were happy to say so when asked. The message was stark. Cricket was a man's game and anybody playing it at international level must bear in mind that if they stayed at the crease making runs they ran the risk of getting their face smashed in.

Since cricket's administration did nothing to curb this policy of blood and iron, the abuse spread. The West Indies, who did not originate either the theory or practice of physical attack, soon realised its advantages. Allowed to bowl their overs at virtually any rate they chose, so that fast bowlers could be kept relatively fresh, they packed their side with talented speed merchants, who consistently pitched short. The cricketing establishment largely confined itself to bewailing the fact that the most beautiful strokes were disappearing from the game and that the helmets batsmen had been forced to don looked unsightly.

As far as this writer is concerned, much of the joy and interest has gone out of Test matches. Granted, there are several reasons for this. Throughout the world groundsmen seem incapable of producing fast, true wickets. The over-rate is too slow and the official levels sometimes set are too lenient. There is no logical reason why teams should not be required to bowl twenty overs per hour. In its greatest days Test cricket was played at a faster pace than that. But it suits nobody's convenience that the game should return to its pristine state. A high over-rate would compel teams to use spin bowlers and who wants to do that, when all the odds are stacked in favour of speed?

But, though other factors have played a part, the toleration of intimidatory fast bowling is at the heart of cricket's sickness. From the time that overarm bowling became legal, fast bowlers have threatened to tilt the balance of the game. In recent years stronger, bigger, fitter fast bowlers, unrestrained by legislators, have destroyed any semblance of balance.

Whether anything can be done is doubtful. Certainly nothing will even be attempted unless the authorities can get some time-honoured nonsense out of their collective head. At the risk of giving offence, which I have no desire to do, I cannot forbear to point at some obstinate fallacies that never seem to die among traditionalists.

Umpires are useless as agents for stamping out the abuse of intimidatory bowling, if they are allowed any discretion in the matter. This has been demonstrated so conclusively that it amazes me that the message has not got through where it might do some good. Administrators can still be heard mumbling about 'the role of the umpire'. Meanwhile, the best fast bowlers in the world can be seen hurling down a succession of bouncers at tail-enders and sometimes hitting them. Anyone who waits for umpires to do something about this under the present laws is highly likely to be disappointed. Not until discretion is taken away from umpires and laws are framed that compel them to act will anything happen.

Perhaps the refusal to face the truth about umpires is part of a wider incomprehension about standards. I would be overjoyed if the game could rely upon the sportsmanship of its participants and the love of spectators for good cricket. But all the pressures of the modern game tend towards winning and providing excitement. There is a pretence that everybody admires the sporting loser, but I do not notice that selection committees show this rare character any mercy.

Intimidatory fast bowling excites crowds. It always has. Many contemporaries pointed out that though Australia was on the receiving end, Australian crowds were gripped by Larwood. He raised the temperature of the game and gave the average spectator full value for his admission money. What many current English spectators are waiting for is a crop of very fast bowlers who can hit West Indian batsmen two or three times an hour. This mayhem would be very popular, especially as there is much frustration at our inability to produce great fast bowlers not separated by thirty-year intervals.

Any action to prohibit intimidation would rob the game of some of its spectacle. I said that we wanted

SNOOKER ROOM
HERE THEY COME!

to see great spinners, but I am afraid I was reflecting the opinion of those who take the niceties of cricket seriously. Those who want only excitement do not object to the spice of violence in the afternoon, particularly if the side they support is dishing it out. So everything depends upon the sort of pleasure that those who control the game wish it to provide.

If the emphasis is going to be placed on excitement and securing a definite result to the exclusion of finesse and style, then I cannot see that cricket is the equal of baseball. Cricket's essential charm surely depends upon its variety and complexity. If spectators no longer appreciate these attributes, then some might argue that it is better that the game should become a minority interest. My opinion is that spectators see so little variety it is hardly surprising we have bred a generation that looks for something else.

Administrators seem to be all at sea in coming to terms with how to maintain cricket's popularity. They insist upon preserving the County Championship in its present form, though few now watch it. To provide the finance the game needs, they tolerate an ever-increasing diet of one-day games where fast bowlers operate under restrictions. Test cricket is the other money-spinner and here fast bowlers do much as they like. Inertia, wishful thinking and commercial pressures are preventing legislators from acting to save what is best in the game.

It is vital to realise that cricket is not developing according to some irreversible evolutionary pattern.

Test cricket is played in the way it is because that is what the regulation of the game permits. It would be transformed if those controlling cricket, in an insane lust for novelty, decreed that it must be played on saturated pitches where the ball turned square. It is the rules that determine how any sport is played. Association football assumed its modern shape only after the off-side law was changed.

There have been too many finicky changes in the laws of cricket, except for the one that is crying out to be made. The authorities ought to recognise that intimidatory bowling has been a murky area throughout the history of the game. What has changed is that contemporary ethics provide no support for the *spirit* of the laws. What is not mandatorily forbidden will be done without regret or shame. Intimidation will stop when the laws adequately penalise it.

I pass no opinion on which of the suggested ways of curbing intimidation is best, because having lacked the skill to play the game even at club level, I do not think I have the experience needed to make a sound judgement. But I do offer one hint to those better qualified. Have you taken note of how many no-balls are bowled by present-day fast bowlers? I know this is because of the front-foot law, but that is not my point. A no-ball concedes one run. Should it? Supposing it conceded four runs, would not that shift the balance a little in favour of slow bowling?

Perhaps a four-run penalty is too severe merely for over-stepping the crease. But if lines are to be drawn across pitches, all my instincts tell me that many bowlers will take chances in the effort to bowl bouncers if the risk is forfeiting one run. They can only be inhibited by their captain telling them that he is not willing to throw away runs prodigally. But is there much point in going any deeper into possible penalties? My guess is that nothing at all is going to be done and that intimidation will be allowed to pursue its increasingly savage course.

Unmixed Blessings

MIKE SEABROOK

WITH RARE EXCEPTIONS, I have always contemplated sports and games with lofty and freezing contempt. Occasionally one chances to find the odd nugget of pure joy amid the prevailing absurdity: I always made a point of watching John McEnroe playing tennis, for example, partly because I find him irresistibly hilarious and partly in the lively expectation of learning at least one new gem for my collection of high-class abuse; I fell instantly in love with the diver who invented the previously unknown style of 'swallow dive with twist, back somersault and glancing head-butt'. The legalised criminal lunacy of boxing was redeemed forever for me when I saw the chap who unleashed the haymaker at his opponent, missed him by several feet and pole-axed the referee, and the same went for football when that Spanish goalkeeper uncoiled himself for a prodigious throw-out and hurled the ball with great force and perfect accuracy back over his head into his own net; and there are many others.

Indeed, just as I have always held that the only sane way to read Shakespeare is by way of the *Oxford Dictionary of Quotations*, whereby you get the good bits without having to sweat through the enormous tracts of tedium, unintelligible jokes and sheer silliness in between, so I have always felt that the only intelligent way to watch most sport is to watch the 'what happened next?' bit on 'A Question of Sport'.

To be serious about sport for a moment, if such a thing is not an intellectual contradiction, I should say that it is a matter of the most sublime and fathomless indifference to me that some idiot has managed to run a mile one second faster than any preceding idiot . . . except that when I am informed, in tones of hushed awe or raving incoherence, reminiscent, respectively, of Sir Alastair Burnett interviewing royalty or Adolf Hitler at a Nuremberg rally, that the same idiot has done the thing in *one hundredth* of a second faster than his predecessor, as if I am expected to take that intelligence seriously, well, that does actually contrive to take us a fathom or so further down still.

The one great exception to this derision with which I contemplate sporting activities is the game of cricket. But what an exception it is. I admit cheerfully to being a clinically certifiable cricket lunatic of the most hopeless and obsessive kind, to my wife's unending despair. Many people, when I have told them that the single reason why I have not gone decades since to live in a civilised country with the French or the Swiss is that there is no cricket there, have gone away shaking their heads sadly and wondering about my sanity (though whether on account of my extreme francophilia or my devotion to cricket or both I have no way of telling). But it's true: cricket is so important a piece of my life that I genuinely could not think of being without it. To me it has always stood for all that makes mankind a decent species to live among – a belief that becomes increasingly difficult to sustain if one considers most of his other activities for very long at a time.

It offers healthy exercise, but in an equally healthy moderation, with none of the frenetic, manic overtones that characterise other athletic activities. It affords an outlet for aggression and the competitive instincts that lurk in men, however civilised, but with none of the sheer, psychotic nastiness that is revealed with depressing inevitability in almost every other organised ball game. Even at international level, with occasional aberrations, it has generally provided a good, combative contest without the participants appearing to feel it necessary to bare their teeth, to cheat or resort to sharp practice, to try to intimidate or physically hurt their opponents, or to deceive or intimidate the umpires – in other words, without any of the ugly manifestations of hatred that are routine in many other human activities.

In one word, cricket has always seemed to me to be the one game that could be described as a *kind* game, where one could still respect one's opponent, whatever he was doing to one for the time being. It's easy to admire an opponent for his skill, his timing, his athleticism, his strength, or whatever form his excellence may take – if you're winning handsomely. Cricket, it has always struck me, is the one game in which most of the players, by tacit but unbreachable convention, are willing to show the same generosity of spirit when the opponent happens to be beating *them* handsomely.

There was an occasion when the great cricketer and greater gentleman Wesley Hall had hurled his forked lightning at Tom Graveney. The batsman had moved, apparently effortlessly, into the correct position, and played one of those sweet, elegant drives that no-one privileged to behold them will ever forget or see the like of again, I suspect. There was a double BANG, the two so close that they sounded almost like a single report. The first was the sound of the ball connecting with Graveney's bat, right in the middle; the second was the ball smashing against the boards beyond the boundary at extra cover, whither it had gone, all along the ground, at what looked like twice the speed at which Hall had delivered it. It hit the board so hard that it rebounded a full thirty yards back into the field. A wonderful moment. But what made it a uniquely *cricketing* moment was what happened next. Wes Hall, applying his air brakes, had pulled up where he got a perfect close-up of this sumptuous stroke. He stood for a moment, watching the ball rocketing away. Then he turned back towards Graveney and slowly, silently, raised both hands above his head, and gravely brought his palms together in three well-spaced, soundless claps. Then he turned, and walked briskly back to his mark to try again, in a profound silence.

The second way in which cricket has always been distinguished for its kindness is in the way it accepts people of very limited ability. No-one is despised by cricketers because he has no talent. If that was the way of the game, I should never have been allowed time to fall head over heels in love with it, because I should have been unceremoniously dumped out of it before I had played half a dozen games. But was I? On the contrary, I have always been made welcome, have made thousands of acquaintances and scores of friends, found a home-from-home everywhere I have been in a fairly well-travelled life, and never, once, been rejected or rebuffed because I had little money and less talent.

Since I eventually decided to take up umpiring, in a desperate quest for *something* I could do well, I have been welcomed, showered with invitations, thanked generously and graciously in what is generally thought of as a pretty thankless role, and honoured by cricketers everywhere. That is not intended as an immodest comment on myself, but a sincere acknowledgement of cricketers' kindness. They accepted me and welcomed me because they saw at first encounter that I was one of their own: I loved the game, I tried to the very limit of my slender ability, I strove to find something I could do properly, and, I hope, I was reasonably agreeable company in the pavilion afterwards.

It's odd, therefore, that this wonderful source of

warmth, companionship and feeling of *belonging* should also provide me with my least-cherished sporting memory of all.

For all that I have said about the game and my love for it, there was a period when I was at school when even cricket was something to be avoided. When I could be found at all on games days, which was rare, given my tenacious powers of passive resistance, I would be driven out to play with a collection of layabouts whose one object was to be all out and beaten as quickly as possible so we could escape to smoke, booze, get to the betting shop, play cards, shoplift and do all the other things that schoolboys prefer to do. We were known as The Bum Set.

One fine summer day when I was in the Sixth Form this disreputable assembly played the Upper Remove, as the form below the sixth was called in those days, and for once we had by some fluke contrived to produce a game that genuinely resembled a real cricket match. This had the unprecedented result that the The Bum Set for once started taking an interest, even to the point of rather wanting to win the match.

Sixth Form dignity would not, of course, tolerate our suffering defeat at the hands of grubby little plebs a full year younger – such differences matter at that time of life. It looked very much as if this was going to happen, however, until our nearest approach to a batsman started making great execution of their slow stuff. He, virtually single-handed, brought us to the position of requiring two runs to win, with one wicket to fall, when the last over came to be bowled.

The Remove's best bowler was brought back, and contained the batsmen until only one ball remained. It was not very fast, but of good length and deadly direction – dead straight, inexorably bound for our hero's wicket. Until, that is, he contrived to get all his legs and pads in its way, plumb in front of his stumps. It was to me, umpiring at the bowler's end after my customary ignominious dismissal, that the Remove bowler had to appeal.

It was out. Of that there was no probable, possible shadow of doubt, no possible doubt whatever. I knew it then and I know it now. Our man was out fairly and squarely and the match was lost. But alas! I hesitated, debating whether I could bring myself to do the wicked thing. Then I did it. I said 'Not out'. I added 'Time'. Then I took off the bails and pulled up the stumps, and hastened off the field, feeling, even as I retreated, more thoroughly ashamed of myself than ever in my life up to that afternoon. I saw that boy's face in my mind throughout the mile and a half trudge back to the changing rooms.

He knew, you see. He knew that I had cheated him. What preoccupied me was that he didn't look angry, or accusing. That would have been bearable. No. He looked as if he was sorry for me. He would have been a schoolboy of rare intuition and sensitivity if that's how he really felt, but that's how he looked, and I have never forgotten it. Since that time I have umpired in the highest class of club cricket, and occasionally at Minor Counties level, and in all that time I have not once given a decision that I knew to be false. That boy did me a service that will stand for a lifetime. But I can still see his face, not accusing but, damningly, *knowing*, and even as I write this, almost twenty-three years after that afternoon, I feel myself flushing hot with shame.

I have not brought this shaming story painfully into the open merely as an act of public self-flagellation, in order to expiate my own demons, or that I may emerge feeling better from the confessional. To do so for those reasons would be a wallow in self-abasement of the most unseemly and revolting kind. I tell it because it illustrates two points. First, I believe that it may serve as a demonstration of the claim I have been making that cricket encourages higher feelings, rather than base ones. For, disgusting and disgraceful though my behaviour was that day, I feel strongly that I am the better for the episode as a whole. It improved me, as a man. The self-loathing that had begun to settle on my shoulders even as I was uprooting the stumps made me think about my private morality in a way that I might never have done otherwise.

The second, more important moral of the tale, though, is its relevance to cricketers generally. For I feel certain that every person who truly adores the game of cricket, everyone who *knows*, in his marrow, what cricket is about, will understand, without any prompting, how I am feeling as I write this account. And ninety-five per cent of them will nod sympathetically,

UMPIRES
I ALWAYS USE PEBBLES MESELF...
CYANIDE TABLETS

and know that they would have felt the same shame, but also the same certainty that they owe the same debt to the game. They will agree that the incident was morally salutary for me, because, had they done what I did, they would have felt as I felt, and become better men for it in the same way. To talk like this, unashamedly linking a ball game with matters of high morality, in the context of any other game, would sound pretentious to the point of absurdity. But cricketers talk in such terms all the time. And, more to the point, they don't foul their game with cheating, because they respect it and love it too much – and because it teaches them not only that playing fairly is more important than winning at all costs, but also that it's much more *fun* that way, as well.

Looked at in that way, it is surprising what disparate, and even apparently downright contradictory, symbols and exemplars the game is capable of producing to bring a mist to the eye of the devotee.

The ways of looking at cricket negatively are numerous and various. 'God, it's so *boring*! Nothing happens!' is one regular plaintive cry from innumerable benighted souls who have yet to fall under its seductive spell. On the other hand there is a vociferous school of thought which holds that these days, at least (and there was never a game like cricket for producing *laudatores temporis acti*), and in the professional game if not elsewhere, there is altogether too *much* happening. They cheat, you will be told. They only desist from cheating when they wish to indulge in sharp practice.

They seek without shame or regret to intimidate opponent and umpire alike. They will lose no opportunity to manufacture a cheap advantage or to exploit one if it should present itself. Well, yes, that is so, to a degree, and I admit, I've said it myself. I've piled diatribe on tirade and tirade on polemic, like Pelion on Ossa and Ossa on Olympus, in my time, lamenting the demise of sportsmanship in favour of its antithesis, gamesmanship.

But the truth of it is that the two depend on each other for their existence, like matter and anti-matter. If the scope for the negative was not there, the positive would have no meaning, for we should have nothing against which to measure it. Cricket, to make the full appeal that, at its best, it makes to the emotions and to sentiment, must needs possess in itself the possibility of its own destruction. If we were not conscious that we had it in our power, by the simple exercise of our will, to pervert the game and turn it into a nasty mirror-image of itself, it would have no power to bring us rejoicing when we reject the temptation to do so.

There is a religious analogy here: an unbeliever may deny the Devil *because* he denies God. As soon as a person accepts God – the word is cognate with 'good', and means the same – he must necessarily embrace the Devil also – that word is a contraction of 'do-evil'. God *needs* the Devil, to provide a measure of his own goodness. But more importantly, believers need him, because religious people deal, in the last resort at least, in certainties; and they need the Devil because the only alternative is a slippage into the agnostic uncertainty with which the rest of us have to come to an accommodation on a daily, *ad hoc* basis as best we can. (It is probably not an accident that many who have not, in the evangelical sense, 'found' cricket accuse cricket devotees of speaking of it as if it was a religion – a charge to which many of the faithful would, of course, give enthusiastic assent.)

All this may sound tortuous and high-flown; but there is a logic in it: rather like saying 'I must at all times carry with me a cyanide tablet, the means of ensuring my certain, irrevocable and instant destruction, in order that I may fully realise and appreciate the joy of continuing life, by not using it. Life would not be as sweet if I hadn't got the pill with me.' And there is something of that in it. If we had not the awful example of international cricket before us at all times, so we could see plain what we might with ease bring our game to, it would be impossible for us to appreciate to the full how much sweeter, how much more fun, how much *nicer* our way of playing the game is.

So turning away from the negative and reflecting on the things that make the game blessed, I can talk of lying under a tree half-asleep on a lazy, golden afternoon, when buying the first ice-cream cornet since one was thirteen becomes an adventure, a half-shamefaced yet irresistible flight back to one's boyhood . . . and in the next breath I can speak of Ian Botham as one of the joys of the game – and have no difficulty in reconciling the two. Yet the one would be seized on by the enemies of the game who denounce it as boring, nothing happening, brain-stem-death enshrined and white-flannelled; whereas the other would be taken as the perfect case in point by the faction who claim that the present-day game represents all that has turned it from a game of grace and manners into a kind of poor-man's gangsterism.

Ian Botham has had a lot of very unfair criticism, most of it from people who are determined to look no further than the surface, and intent at that on seeing only the bad, the slatternly and the oafish. To be sure, he has been guilty of minor misbehaviour – of kinds that go naturally with the perennial naughty schoolboy who is undoubtedly bottled up inside the man, and needs little excuse to come bubbling and clamouring out. He has sometimes been petulant, silly, and occasionally downright boorish. But he has been those things, mostly, in private, and they would have been forgotten had his privacy not been invaded. Often, indeed, he has done no more than react in the way that most normally red-blooded men would react to given provocation. It's rather like the way spiky individualist characters like Norman Tebbit, or Ken Livingstone, or Lord Denning, often enunciate what others feel but keep quiet about.

So, for example, if I was in the middle of a flaming row with someone on an aeroplane and some stranger butted in to tell me to behave myself, I, in the excitement of the moment, would probably tell him to piss off in no uncertain terms. I might not go as far as Botham, not least because I haven't got his fearlessness. If I was treated by the rabid end of the press as he has been, I'd most assuredly react the same way. The problem Botham has had to find his own way of dealing with this has been that he is judged by the standards of people who are able, because of their anonymity, to be normal, while he himself, because of his prodigious talents and the flamboyant, extravagant generosity with which he spends them, is quite unable to be very normal. It is to his great credit that he *has* found a way of dealing with the problem, and seems to have found himself a good measure of equilibrium and repose in the process. There is a bigness about him which I find wholly absent from most of his detractors. He may be a silly ass from time to time, but there's nothing of the weasel about him. If he is that naughty schoolboy, he has the virtue of being a lovable one: his naughtiness is mischievousness and high spirits, not evil; and there's a generosity, a decency and a common humanity in him which I don't see in many of his cold-eyed, thin-lipped critics.

His cricket speaks of all this, most eloquently. How often, these days, do you see professional games players look as if they're *enjoying* themselves, as if they're actually having fun? Botham looks like that most of the time. At his best he plays the game with a simple, buoyant exuberance – and that signifies, to any real lover of the game, a generosity of spirit. He has this tremendous gift, and he showers it lavishly all about him – on his team, on the opposition, on us watching.

He believes, quite visibly, that the game in essence is a simple affair. But this is not to say, as some have said, that he is a simple person. I don't know him personally, so I could be wrong, but he doesn't strike me as a simple man, but a rather complex one, with far more to him than is commonly credited. But he has been stereotyped, by his admirers as much, in their different way, as by his detractors. I think he and cricket go well together. I think he would understand exactly what I was getting at in my story about The Bum Set, and I think he would agree with my conclusions.

And yet . . . and yet Ian Botham is one of those who regularly proclaims a message that is the very opposite of another proposition I've made in this essay. He says, forcefully, that we should be more concerned with winning, that we English, in our cricket and elsewhere in our national life, have made far too much of the cult of the gallant 'good loser', when we should have been out there red in tooth and claw, being winners. Winning, I have heard him say often, is what should be celebrated, not losing gracefully. There's nothing virtuous in coming second. Words to that effect. But, if he and I could discuss it at the length such a question would require, I don't think we would find ourselves too far apart.

I suspect that what he means is that there's nothing commendable in a wimpish lack of fight – in the kind of fastidious disdain to soil one's hands with combat that one has seen sometimes in our sporting representatives. And I'd agree with that whole-heartedly. Botham would regard that kind of foppish, superior disdain for the fray as deeply contemptible, and so would I. But cricket was *never* like that, except in the wandering minds of sentimental old gentlemen who had taken Newbolt far too seriously, and misunderstood even Newbolt, at that. Anyone who sets foot on a cricket field not wanting to win, and determined to win if he can do so fairly, has no right to be there. He should take up a solitary pastime immediately. For cricket is above all else competitive, and so it is treated by any and all who truly understand and love it, live it and breathe it. But there is no incompatibility between this statement and all the other claims I have made for it that it is a kindly, tolerant and friendly game. The man who steps onto the field with the attitude I have just stigmatised betrays the game, because in that attitude he reveals a contempt for his own team-mates and his opponents equally, and there is no place for him.

The catalyst that permits this co-existence of high competitiveness with friendliness, kindness and so on, is *fairness*. There is a language-wide difference between saying, on the one hand, that you must desire and be determined to win, and saying, on the other, that you must be determined to win *at all costs*. You must, and you must not, respectively. The two are thus reconcilable – just as it is entirely proper to insist, on the one hand, that we must have a free press but that, on the other hand, that in no way confers legitimacy on any notion that that same press is entitled to tell lies about people. The notion of freedom of the press and that of extreme sanctions against publication of lies, so far from being incompatible, imply and require each other; the freer the press is, the greater its responsibility to be scrupulous in the eschewal of lies – an analogy with Newton's third law which is amply demonstrated by the fact that the vilest, most lying rag in newspaper history was the *Völkischer Beobachter*. No contemporary British parallel need be adduced; but I should imagine that Ian Botham, who has suffered grievously at the hands of some newspapers, would agree with me about this, as he would also, I believe, about the cricketing paradox that introduced this digression.

At the opposite end of the cricketing spectrum from Ian Botham, the joy of the game encompasses games at the fag-end of the club season. They always seem to be at pretty grounds like North Mymms – a friendly club which inspired my first words in print – and they are always tinged with a faint air of melancholy. The air is chilly, there always seems to be a threat of rain which never quite materialises, the fine drizzle whipped away by a high wind before it can make you feel wet, so that you are always surprised when you get into the pavilion for tea to find suddenly how wet you actually *are*. The sky is always a fast-racing armada of low clouds in a thousand gradations of grey, and there's often a monarchical elm in one corner of the ground, with great swirling cascades of yellowing leaves erupting into the air, and windswept rooks taking off from the topmost twigs like blown scraps of black fabric.

When the sun comes out at these games it always

has that special old-goldy, antique light, a stormy light that somehow makes the air seem to swim; and there is something in the quality of the air at this end of the season which somehow alters the sound of the bat on the ball, a sound as unmistakable for any other in the world as distant churchbells or the high-pitched whistle of the old steam engines that used to send a quiver of expectation through small boys sitting by the lineside, back in days when trains were *trains*. In summer the 'thock' of the bat on the ball is a joyous, triumphant sound, all high optimism and expectancy; but in these late matches in autumn, almost winter, it has a way of sounding almost wistful. But I expect it's only the mood transferring itself to the sensations.

Lord's is a holy place which contrives to be at its very best at whatever time of the year you visit it, but for me it, too, is a winter place. Walking through the Grace Gates on a dismal Monday, with St John's Wood pavements streaming and reflecting the lights of the traffic, is like inhaling some illegal substance and being transported to a nicer, safer world – and the oddest thing is that, actually, it seems far more real than the sad London you've left outside. Just walking round under the covered part behind the free seats, looking wistfully at the Long Stop and wishing it was open (I wish I could discover the secret of why it's *always* closed when I pass it), you can hear whatever your own version of the soundless-clapping host happens to be.

For no reason accountable to science, when I go to

Lord's in the winter I daydream always of dark cherry-red caps and West Indians, in particular of Frank Worrell, batting like a dark-brown Tom Graveney back in 1963, when I made my Lord's and Test match debut as a timid thirteen-year-old, stricken and overwhelmed with awe - of the place, the sense of history and hallowed sanctity, and the sheer impossible reality that I, a poor kid from a village, was *there*, beholding titans, who, to be honest, I'd never really been able to convince myself actually existed.

When I go there in spring, on the other hand, I can see no other image in my mind's eye than Dennis Lillee clean bowling the saintly Geoff Boycott for, I believe, eleven, with a ball that he clearly never saw, and the stump flying yards back towards the impossibly distant wicket-keeper – a case of Ormazd and Ahriman, Osiris and Seth, if ever there was one.

And these days, when I go there in the summer, it's for Eton and Harrow with pints of Pimms at the Tavern, or the last day of a County game that is already written off as a draw. I people the place with roaring thousands in imagination, but when I'm there in the flesh I find that I wish to be alone.

These are some images of the most blessed of games, the only one that has ever exerted a hold on me, but one that draws me like the tide. They are taken at random from among many others, all as varied as these unrepresentative few. Reading John Arlott – especially *The Echoing Green*, his best book by far – Cardus and Robertson-Glasgow, Siegfried Sassoon and A.G. Macdonnell, A.A. Thomson and Blunden and de Selincourt, and simply sitting in a warm room with the wind lashing rain against the bow window, thinking about cricket, are sources of warm, undemanding pleasure, which can be savoured alone or companionably, mostly in silence, with a bottle of Burgundy and an initiated friend. Watching promising youngsters grow and fill out, putting on their strength and hitting their first fifty, and then their first hundred.

But if I had to choose the deepest, quietest but most potent blessing of all that the game has to bestow, I should nominate two. One is the meeting of old friends – fierce and uncompromising rivals first, and then, in the pavilion afterwards, just good friends, who have been presented with the same silver key and who speak the same language, quiet and undemonstrative, with a whole year's life passed since you saw them last to ask about and tell about. It doesn't happen every week – no-one was ever born so fortunate and the soul would not withstand it if it did. But if you're lucky, it happens several times a season, and, if you're willing, it can keep you feeling young a long way beyond your span. The second is the quiet satisfaction of knowing you're in love with the only game in the world that can, genuinely, make you a better person for loving it.